HİZMET

HİZMET

Questions and Answers on the Gülen Movement

Muhammed Çetin

15 14 13 12   1 2 3 4

Published by Blue Dome Press
244 Fifth Avenue #2HS
New York, NY 10001

www.bluedomepress.com

Library of Congress Cataloging-in-Publication Data Available

ISBN: 978-1-935295-17-4

Printed by
Ayhan Matbaası , Istanbul - Turkey

Contents

List of Questions

Media

Dialogue Platforms

MOBILIZATION

Is Hizmet a Sect or Cult?

Is Hizmet Conflictual or Violent?

Is Hizmet Anachronistic?

EFFICACY OF HIZMET

PREFACE

This book is about a contemporary social phenomenon, variously referred to as "Hizmet" or "the Volunteers' movement." In academic circles it is often called "the Gülen Movement", taking the name of the person who inspired it, Fethullah Gülen.

Gülen is one of the world's most influential Islamic scholars of his generation. The author of more than fifty books, Gülen has dedicated his life to promoting peaceful interrelationship within and between different communities, societies, cultures and religious traditions.

Since the 1970s the social movement he inspires has grown into a transnational educational, inter-cultural and interfaith movement, with participants numbering in the millions. Participants have founded and run hundreds of modern educational institutions, as well as print and broadcast media outlets and dialogue societies on every continent. The movement has therefore attracted a great deal of academic attention, in recent years.

In 2009 my own sociological research and analysis of the Movement was published in the book *The Gülen Movement: Civic Service without Borders* (Blue Dome). Following that publication I was asked by many readers to make the same information available to a wider audience. To that end I have attempted to represent what I found in my research in a question-answer format stripped of sociological jargon as far as possible. It is my sincere hope that this effort will make knowledge about the Movement and the Movement itself more accessible to those very people who commit to self-sacrifice and serving others in Hizmet and other peaceful civil society movements all over the world; that is, it has been written for all concerned, caring, peaceful citizens of whatever nation.

INTRODUCTION

1. What is this book about?

This book is about a contemporary social phenomenon which is known by a number of different names: "the Volunteers' Movement", "the Service Movement" or just "Hizmet." Also, researchers and journalists often refer to it as "the Gülen Movement", using the name of the Islamic scholar who inspired the Movement, Fethullah Gülen.

In this book these names are used interchangeably; wherever 'Movement' is used with a capital letter it refers to this particular social movement (i.e., Hizmet), and wherever the word 'movement' is not capitalized, it is being used to refer to social movements in general.

2. What does the word "hizmet" mean?

"Hizmet" is the Turkish word for "service" and is the term most commonly used by participants for the Movement.

3. Why is this book needed?

Hizmet has attracted a great deal of academic attention in recent years, but more studies are still needed to describe it fully and accurately. This book is intended to summarize and represent the conclusions of much of that academic work in a manner more easily accessible to the lay person or non-specialist.

4. When did Hizmet start as a movement?

The Movement originated in 1970s' Turkey as a faith-inspired initiative to improve educational opportunities for a local community; since then, it has grown into a transnational educational, inter-cultural and interfaith movement. It is estimated that participants number in several millions. Hizmet has securely established, respected institutions (of different kinds, but mostly schools) on every continent.

5. What is the particular attraction of studying Hizmet?

Its attraction lies in its potential to show the capacity of an Islam-inspired movement to mobilize huge numbers of religiously-minded and observant individuals not only to accept but to *cherish* a secular, pluralist, democratic social and political order.

6. How can studying the Movement help people who are not taking part in it?

A clear understanding of this particular Movement can help other cultural actors and peaceful movements to expand their repertoires of action for societal peace and inter-civilizational co-operation. Learning about the Movement can contribute to the vitality of civil society, and it may help to diminish polarization and fragmentation in Turkey and similar societies.

7. What previous research has been done on similar movements?

There has been little research into peaceful, faith-inspired social movements arising from Islamic backgrounds. Most studies overlook the presence of non-political elements in emergent movements. They totally ignore themes such as philanthropy, altruism and voluntarism which help explain the dynamics of participation in activities that do not directly benefit those taking part. Such studies fail to address the reasons why (and how) faith – Islam in the case of Hizmet – meets the need for cultural or political empowerment.

8. Is faith really a factor in the development of social movements?

Yes, faith and empowerment by it form a substantial part of civic society and democracy. Faith and empowerment contribute significantly to preserving and developing volunteerism and dialogue. They help to build relationships to achieve shared goals. They encourage people to compete to do good and to provide non-materialistic and non-contentious services. Religious experience involves meanings, values and experience other than those entertained in protest theories or conflictual political actions. The real social significance of these factors needs to be acknowledged as affecting people's views, choices and actions.

Religious experience or its influences are located at the heart of all societies. Faith is a motivating force. It helps to build relationships of trust or "social capital" for peaceful civil society movements. It does not only produce conflictual relationships. Faith cannot always be discounted or analyzed in terms of something other than itself. Faith and empowerment by it are not a dependent variable, determined and structured by the social, economic, and political conditions; so religious experience cannot be dismissed as a proxy or substitute for something else such as direct or contentious political action. It cannot just be "explained away" in terms of social, psychological and other material goals such as conflict-evading pacifism, etc.

9. What is the place of moral and spiritual values in the study of Hizmet?

Since Hizmet originated as a faith-inspired civil society movement, motivations for participation include spiritual resources and moral values drawn from the Islamic tradition, like altruism and other nonmaterial incentives.

10. Why is it useful to know about the thought of the participants in the Movement and not just their activities?

Their action and their own interpretations of service could helpfully inform a variety of discussions of social and religious forces related to Islam and peaceful Muslim social or cultural movements. Learning about them may also shed light on circumstances and issues in the recent history of Turkey.

11. What makes Hizmet different from movements of the past and present in Europe?

Although Hizmet is a contemporary movement, it concerns itself with forms of action, content and meanings that are qualitatively different from the tradition of struggle frequently seen in European societies. It does not fit into the conventional categories of the workers' movement of industrial capitalism and modern leftist movements.

Along with inequalities or changes in society that are economic and political, there are changes and meanings that arise because of the various contractions of the fields in which cultural and moral values can be expressed. Meanings and values such as faith, family, morality, and parts of people's history have been or are being sidelined or forgotten. Many mechanisms of self-control and autonomy, especially those arising from people's cultural heritage and religion have been pushed out by modernity. Their constructive influence has lessened, and they have contracted to become mere expressions of individualism or escapism.

Hizmet recognizes the need for a new and inclusive synthesis arising from the past but based upon universal values and modern realities. The Movement therefore emphasizes a different array of factors, including values, such as equality, freedom, dignity, altruism, good life, ecology and morality; these are needs and issues which the current and prevalent socio-political structure mostly fails to implement.

12. Why is Hizmet important for social movement researchers who are accustomed to examining the movements of Europe and North America?

Faith-inspired movements, especially Islamic ones, can be very different from the social movements that sociologists and political scientists have previously analyzed. So, to avoid reductionism, studying such faith-inspired movements requires a focus shift from social movement researchers who are accustomed to examining the protest movements and political understanding of Europe or North America.

13. What is reductionism and what are its dangers when discussing social movements?

Social, political, economic or methodological reductionism occurs when researchers offer at best a partial explanation of collective action. It is unsatisfactory because it does not take account of or distorts key aspects of a movement and its history; for example, it may treat philanthropic services and culturally innovative potential as politically subversive when they are not.

14. How can studying Hizmet contribute to academia and knowledge in general?

Studying it can improve our ability to analyze future events and to resolve contradictory socio-political analyses of Turkey and the region. It may also contribute to our understanding of contemporary social movements and their potential.

THE HISTORY OF HIZMET

15. What is the significance of the history or socio-political context to the rise of movements in Turkey?

To understand contemporary social phenomena in Turkey, we need to understand the changing circumstances in which the attempt was made to establish and then hold on to a nationalist, *laicist* and Westernized republic after the end of the Ottoman Empire.

For the emergence, dynamics and outcomes of any social movement (especially in the case of a multi-purpose civic action like Hizmet), the political system, its institutions and processes, and the larger social and cultural ethos are highly significant material factors.

16. Can the rise of Hizmet in Turkey be attributed to the economic and political liberalization policies of Prime Minister Turgut Özal (1983–93)?

No, it cannot. For a movement to rise and develop very many determinants are at work, and movements cannot be reduced to one determinant. Different movements arise out of unique combinations of different factors: the historical context, grievances, economy, norms, class, beliefs, resources, networks, strategies, ideology, organizations, leadership, adversary, etc.

Explanations focusing on a particular event or events may contain a small kernel of truth, but they miss the reality and meaning of Hizmet. For example, it is at best a very partial explanation to claim that the Movement emerged because of increased migration from the countryside to the cities, the urbanization, industrialization and modernization of Turkey during the Özal decade. This sort of explanation is unsatisfactory because it fails to take account of or distorts key aspects of the Movement and its history.

In fact, Özal himself was from the faith communities. He was one of the many people who were already educated, qualified and holding roles and status in Turkish society and the state structure at that time. There were already other state bodies functioning independently, and there was in place a large and strong protectionist opposition to what Özal said, planned and carried out. So a single individual, by coming to a higher position one day, could not have produced a large number of educated and qualified people like that in such a short period of time, let alone a movement like Hizmet. The reality is that the faith-inspired communities had already started to use all the different forms of communication networks and media. Furthermore, as entrepreneurs who were independent of state subsidy, they had already proved themselves successful in foreign-exchange-earning export industries.

Social movements take time to develop; they do not come ready made. In any case, the availability of political opportunities does not automatically and promptly translate into increased action and is *insufficient* to account for the emergence of a collective action and actor. For an organized collective action as large as Hizmet, there has to be, already in place, a sufficient number of people with the necessary intellectual and professional skills, and the readiness and will to be employed *before* a window of opportunity opens up in history.

Generally, a collective actor or action (such as a social movement or political party) does not automatically spring from political or social tensions or conditions. Numerous factors determine whether or not this will occur. Necessary factors include the availability of adequate organizational resources, the ability of movement leaders to represent their ideology attractively to the public or masses, and a political context which makes action possible.

In short, to say that Hizmet emerged because of Turgut Özal's policies, or any other specific event, ignores the fact that informal networks and everyday solidarity circles already existed; it disregards the widespread and strong networks that people already belonged to; it overlooks the fact that individuals and groups had already accumulated many experiences of living and working together for specific purposes. The Movement already had resources for mobilization. These resources were ready to be directed towards new goals because they were already in place. Had they not been, the situation could not have created them, nor could the Movement have benefited from the situation to redirect and reshape its action.

17. Did the Movement's cultural networks exist before the Movement's public appearance?

Yes. We need to distinguish between the discovery of the Movement by the mass media and its organizational and cultural origins. Prior to the 1980 military coup, Hizmet participants had already responded to the crisis in education by setting up institutions such as student halls of residence, university entrance courses, and teacher associations. They had also started to address the contraction in the field for the expression of moral concerns in the public arena by establishing publishing houses and a journal.

18. Did the Movement emerge because of a religious conflict in Turkey?

No. It did not emerge because of any conflict, nor as the expression of a conflict, let alone one between the religious-minded and the secularists in Turkey. Some of those who oppose the Movement for their own ideological reasons try to portray any effort from the faith-inspired communities as reactionary or fundamentalist, but Hizmet has never been connected with any anarchy, terror or misuse of office. Any attempts to label or describe the Movement in this way have no concrete basis, and the Turkish public and the courts have rejected all such allegations. The overwhelming majority in Turkey does not see the Movement as fundamentalist, nor as posing any threat to existing political or economic institutions.

GÜLEN AND THE FORMATIVE YEARS OF HIZMET

19. When and where was Fethullah Gülen born?

Fethullah Gülen was born in a village in Erzurum, eastern Anatolia in 1941. His date of birth on his national identification card and his passport is 1941.

20. What form did his early education take?

There were few opportunities for a general secular education for ordinary Turkish people at this time so his parents took charge of his early education and religious instruction. Gülen's parents sent him to the nearest state primary school for three years. However, because his father was later assigned by the state to a post as preacher and imam in another town, one that had no secondary school, Gülen was unable to progress to secondary education.

Although at this time mosques and congregational prayer were permitted by law, all other forms of religious instruction and practice were not. Even so, Gülen's parents, like many other ordinary Turkish people, kept up the Turkish Islamic tradition and made sure that their children learned the Qur'an and basic religious practices, including prayer. They avoided confrontation with the authorities and the regime, concealing the fact that they were providing elementary Islamic instruction to their own and their neighbors' children.

21. What was Gülen's education and training during his youth?

During this decade (1950–60) Fethullah Gülen completed his religious education and training under various prominent scholars and Sufi masters leading to the traditional Islamic *ijaza* (license to teach). This education was provided almost entirely within an informal system, tacitly ignored and unsupported by the state and running parallel to its education system. At the same time, Gülen pursued and completed his secondary-level secular education through external exams.

In 1958–9, he sat for and passed the state exam to become an imam and preacher. On the basis of the exam result he was assigned by the state to the very prestigious posting in Edirne.

In the late 1950s, he encountered and studied compilations of the scholarly work *Risale-i Nur* (Epistles of Light series) by Said Nursi, but he never met its famous author.

22. Who was Said Nursi? Why did he become famous?

He was the most important Islamic thinker of the Republican era. Nursi was an Islamic modernist whose writings mapped out an accommodation between the ideas of constitutional democracy and individual liberty and religious faith.

During the First World War Nursi fought against foreign invasion and for independence and spoke out against both modern Islamic authoritarianism and economic and political backwardness and separatism. His ideas for a modern Islamic consciousness emphasize the need for a significant role for religious belief in public life. He objected to withholding knowledge, whether religious or scientific, from the general public, and he embraced scientific and technological development.

Although he was not involved in any rebellions, the Independence Tribunals of the early years of the Republic sentenced him to exile in western Anatolia for his religious activities.

23. What were Gülen's formative experiences in the development of his own leadership?

Throughout his service in Edirne Gülen maintained a devout asceticism while mixing with people and remaining on good terms with the civic and military authorities he encountered. He witnessed how the youth were being attracted to extremist, radical ideologies, and strove through his preaching to draw them away from such ideas. Using his own money, he would buy and distribute published materials to counter atheistic communism and an aggressively militant atheism. He saw the erosion of traditional moral values among the youth and the educated sector of Turkish society. This erosion was feeding criminality and political and societal conflict. These observations and experiences were formative influences on Gülen's intellectual and community leadership and reinforced his faith in the meaning and value of human beings and life.

24. Were there any influences other than Turkish or Islamic on the development of Gülen's view of the world?

In 1961 Gülen was sent to Iskenderun as part of his compulsory military service. His commanding officer assigned to him the duty of lecturing soldiers on faith and morality. Recognizing Gülen's intellectual ability, the officer gave him many Western classics to read. Throughout his military service Gülen maintained his simple, ascetic lifestyle.

In 1963, following military service, Gülen gave a series of lectures in Erzurum on Jalaladdin Rumi and moral issues.

25. How was Gülen treated by the Turkish state during his service as imam?

In 1964, he was assigned a new post in Edirne, where he became very influential among the educated youth and ordinary people. The militantly *laicist* authorities were displeased by his having such influence and wanted him dismissed. Before they could bring this about, Gülen had himself assigned to another city, Kırklareli, in 1965. There, after working hours, he organized evening lectures and talks. In this phase of his career, just as before, he took no active part in party politics and taught only about moral values in personal and collective affairs.

26. Where and how did Gülen's ideas on education and service to the community take form?

In 1966, Yaşar Tunagür, who had known Gülen from earlier in his career, became deputy head of the country's Directorate of Religious Affairs. On assuming his position in Ankara, Tunagür assigned Gülen to the post that he himself had just vacated in Izmir on the Aegean coast.

On March 11, Gülen was transferred to the Izmir region, where he held managerial responsibility for a mosque, a student study and boarding-hall, and for preaching in the Aegean region. He continued to live ascetically. For almost five years he lived in a tiny hut near the Kestanepazarı Hall and took no wages for his services.

It was during these years that Gülen's ideas on education and service to the community began to mature and take definite form. From 1969 he set up meetings in coffee houses, lecturing all around the provinces and in the villages of the region. He also organized summer camps for middle and high school students.

27. What happened to Gülen in the military coup of 1970?

Upon the March 12, 1970 military coup, a number of prominent Muslims in Izmir, who had supported Kestanepazarı Hall and associated activities for the region's youth, were arrested. On May 1, Gülen too was arrested and he was held for six months without charge until his release on November 9. Later, all the others associated with the hall were also released, also without charge.

When asked later to explain these arrests, the authorities said that they had arrested so many leftists that they felt they needed to arrest some prominent Muslims in order to avoid being accused of unfairness. They released Gülen on condition that he give no more public lectures.

28. Did the arrests frighten Gülen and those around him into reducing their activities?

No. In 1971, Gülen left his post and Kestanepazarı Hall but retained his status as a state-authorized preacher. He began setting up more study rooms and boarding halls in the Aegean region: the funding for these came from local people. It is at this point that a particular group of about one hundred people began to be visible as a service group, that is, a group gathered around Gülen's understanding of service to the community and positive action.

29. Why and how did Gülen focus on education as a theme of his teaching and activities?

Between 1972 and 1975, Gülen held the post of preacher in several cities in the Aegean and Marmara regions. He continued to preach and to teach the ideas about education and the service ethic that he had developed. He continued setting up hostels for high school and university students. At this time educational opportunities were still scarce for ordinary Anatolian people. Most student accommodation in the major cities was controlled or infiltrated by extreme leftists and rightists and seethed in a hyper-politicized atmosphere. Parents in provincial towns whose children had passed entrance examinations for universities or city high schools were caught in a dilemma – to surrender their children's care to the ideologues or to deny them further education and keep them at home.

The hostels set up by Gülen and his companions offered parents the chance to send their children to the big cities to continue their secular education, while protecting them from the hyper-politicized environment.

30. How did Gülen raise the funds for the services in the 1970s?

To support these educational efforts, people who shared Gülen's service ethic now set up a system of bursaries for students. The funding for the hostels and bursaries came entirely from local communities in which Gülen's service-ethic idea (*hizmet*) was spreading steadily.

31. How did Gülen's new type of community action start to become widespread?

With Gülen's encouragement, around his discourse of positive action and responsibility, ordinary people were starting to mobilize. They wished to counteract the effects of violent ideologies and the ensuing social and political disorder on their own children and on youth in general. Students in the hostels also began to play a part in spreading the discourse of service and positive action. Periodically, they returned to their home towns and visited surrounding towns and villages. Talking of their experiences and the ideas they had encountered, they consciously diffused the *hizmet* idea in the region.

Since 1966, Gülen's talks and lectures had been recorded on audio cassettes and distributed throughout Turkey. Thus, the already existing networks of relations, this new type of community action, the students' activities, and the new technology of communication all contributed to the rapid nationwide spread of the *hizmet* discourse.

32. When and how did the first stage of the institutionalization of the services and the Movement take place?

In 1974, the first university preparatory courses were established in Manisa, where Gülen was posted at the time. Until then, it had been largely the children of very wealthy and privileged families who had had access to university education. The new courses in Manisa offered the hope that in future there might be better opportunities for children from ordinary Anatolian families. The idea took hold that, if properly supported, the children of ordinary families could take up and succeed in higher education.

Word spread of these achievements, and the following year Gülen was invited to speak at a series of lectures all over Turkey. The service idea became firmly rooted in various cities and regions of the country. From this time on, the country-wide mobilization of people drawn to support education and non-political altruistic services can be called a movement.

33. What was Gülen's response to the politicization and chaos of the late 1970s in Turkey?

In 1976, the Religious Directorate posted Gülen to Bornova, Izmir. Izmir was the site of one of Turkey's major universities with a correspondingly large student population and a great deal of the militant activism typical of universities in the 1970s.

It came to Gülen's attention that leftist groups were running protection rackets to extort money from small businessmen and shopkeepers in the city and deliberately disrupting the business and social life of the community. The racketeers had already murdered a number of their victims. In his sermons, Gülen spoke out and urged those being threatened by the rackets neither to yield to threats and violence, nor to react with violence and exacerbate the situation. He urged them to report the crimes to the police and have the racketeers dealt with through the proper channels. This message led to threats being made against his life.

At the same time, he challenged the students of left and right to come to the mosque and discuss their ideas with him. He offered to answer any questions, whether secular or religious, which they put to him. A great many students took up this offer. So, in addition to his daily duties giving traditional religious instruction and preaching, Gülen devoted every Sunday evening to these discussion sessions.

34. Did Gülen make any contribution to the lives of people outside Turkey at that time?

In 1977, he traveled in northern Europe, visiting and preaching among Turkish communities to raise their consciousness about values and education. He encouraged them in the *hizmet* ethic of positive action and altruistic service. He advised them both to preserve their cultural and religious values and to integrate into their host societies.

35. Were Gülen's efforts always opposed by the authorities?

No. His efforts also elicited positive responses from many in authority. By the age of thirty-six, Gülen had become one of the three most widely recognized and influential preachers in Turkey. For example, in 1977, when the prime minister, other ministers and state dignitaries came to a Friday prayer in the Blue Mosque in Istanbul, a politically sensitive occasion in Turkey, Gülen was invited to preach.

36. How did Gülen appeal to the masses?

Gülen encouraged participants in the Movement to go into publishing. Some of his articles and lectures were published as anthologies. In the late 1970s a group of teachers inspired by his ideas established the Teachers' Foundation to support education and students.

In 1979, the Teachers' Foundation started its own monthly journal, *Sızıntı*, which became the highest selling monthly in Turkey. In terms of genre, it was a pioneering venture, being a magazine of sciences, humanities, faith, and literature. Its publishing mission was to show that science and religion were not incompatible and that knowledge of both was necessary to be successful in this life.

Since *Sızıntı*'s foundation, every month Gülen has contributed an editorial and a section about the spiritual or inner aspects of Islam (Sufism), and the meaning of faith in modern life.

37. How did Gülen urge individuals to serve society constructively?

In Turkey up to the 1980s hyperpoliticization of all issues in society and artificial divisions between people were prevalent. Extremist and ideological issues were raised between rightists and leftists, around the sectarian division between Alevis and Sunnis, around the ethnic distinction between the Turkish and Kurdish, and later around differing definitions of secularism between the *laicists* and the religious-minded. Such issues dominated society so much that tensions and fights began to undermine its security and stability, even indeed its survival. Thousands of people were killed.

Throughout this period, Gülen, as scholar, writer, preacher and civil society leader, strove to draw people out of societal tension and conflict. His message reached the masses through audio and video cassettes, as well as public lectures and private meetings. He appealed to people not to become part of on-going partisan conflictual issues and ideological fights. He analyzed the prevalent conditions and the ideologies behind the societal violence, terror and clashes. He applied his scholarship and his intellectual and personal resources to convince others (notably, young university students) that they need not resort to violence, terror and destruction to establish a progressive, prosperous and peaceful society.

He maintained that violence, terrorism, death, ignorance, moral decay and corruption could be overcome through forbearance and compassion, through conversation, interaction, education and co-operation. He reminded them not to expect everything from the system because of its backwardness in some respects, its stifling bureaucratic, partisan and procedural stagnation, and its lack of qualified personnel. He urged people instead to use their constitutionally given rights to contribute to and serve society constructively and altruistically. In addition, he convinced them that such service is both the means and the end of being a good person, a good citizen and a good believer.

38. How did he impart his understanding of the service ethic to the wider public?

Gülen started to talk to people from all walks of life in Turkey. He visited individuals, groups, cafes, small villages, towns and metropolitan cities. From street peddlers to industrialists and exporters, from secondary school students to postgraduates and faculty, from the common people to leading figures and elites, he imparted the same message to all: sound education and institutionalization, and to achieve that, altruistic contribution and services. He appealed to values that are present in all traditions and religions: duty, moral obligation, disinterested contribution, voluntary philanthropism and altruistic services.

His listeners set up student hostels, primary, secondary and high schools, universities, study centers, college-preparatory courses, press and media organs, publishing houses, student bursaries and research scholarships. The Movement participants played a modernizing role in the educational field. Their behavior towards the outside world translated into institutional support or an advanced form of cooperative social enterprise.

Gülen genuinely believes in and encourages free enterprise. According to him, believers both in Turkey and abroad must be wealthy. He emphasizes education hand in hand with development, and economic and cultural togetherness. He recommends knowledge against ignorance, work against poverty, and solidarity and cohesion against disunity and schism.

39. What was Gülen's response to the violence and terror of the 1980s in Turkey?

In February 1980, Gülen gave a series of lectures which were attended by thousands of people. In them he preached against violence, anarchy and terror. Recordings of the lectures were distributed widely on audio cassette.

40. Why had an autonomous civic culture not developed in Turkey by the 1980s?

In Turkey, the primacy given to party-political struggle has thwarted the potential for innovation present in society; it has prevented the development of an autonomous civic culture. It has also blocked the development of a deeply-felt identification by the public with democratic institutions.

41. How did Gülen judge the hyperpoliticization of nonpolitical issues in Turkey?

Although he was not himself involved in any political movements, as a teacher and preacher Gülen engaged actively with individuals embedded in the culture of leftist and rightist movements. He realized that the artificial hyperpoliticization of nonpolitical issues distorted and dissolved many things into violence. He witnessed crises in the political movements that resulted in an escalation of terrorist activity.

He maintained that in such situations where brute force is offered as a solution to problems, "it is impossible to speak of intellect, judgment, rights, justice, or law. On the contrary, in their stead, is unlawfulness, injustice and oppression."

42. What happened to Gülen at the time of the 1980 military coup?

In 1980, on September 5, Gülen spoke from the pulpit before taking leave of absence for the next twenty days because of illness.

On September 12, the day of the military coup, his home was raided. He was not detained as he was not at home. He requested another leave of absence for forty-five days. Then the house where he was staying as a guest was raided and he was detained. After a six-hour interrogation, he was released.

On November 25, he was transferred to Çanakkale. However, due to illness again, he was not able to serve there. From March 20, 1981, he took indefinite leave of absence.

43. What was the response of the Turkish people to the 1980 coup?

Before, during and after the two previous coups in 1960 and 1974, there had been growing public unrest, bombings, assassinations, riots and orchestrated street fighting between conflicting groups. By the third coup, the Turkish public had learned to stay calm. There was no visible public reaction.

44. What was the response of the faith communities and Hizmet to the 1980 coup?

The faith communities, including Hizmet, continued with their lawful and peaceful activities without drawing any extra attention to themselves. Gülen and the Movement avoided large public gatherings but continued to promote the service ethic through publishing and small meetings.

At this point, the Movement turned again to the use of technology. For the first time in Turkey a preacher's talks were recorded and distributed on videotape.

In spite of the coup, the Movement continued to grow and act successfully. In 1982, Movement participants set up a private high school, Yamanlar Koleji in Izmir.

45. Why did Gülen stop lecturing and preaching to the masses after the 1980s?

In 1989, Gülen was approached by the Directorate of Religious Affairs and asked to resume his duties. His license was reinstated to enable him to serve as an Emeritus Preacher with the right to preach in any mosque in Turkey. Between 1989 and 1991, he preached in Istanbul on Fridays and on alternate Sundays in Istanbul and Izmir in the largest mosques in the cities. His sermons drew crowds in the tens of thousands, numbers unprecedented in Turkish history. These sermons were videotaped and also broadcast.

At the beginning of the 1990s, the police uncovered a number of conspiracies by marginal militant Islamists and other small ideological groups to assassinate Gülen. These groups also placed *agents provocateurs* in the areas around the mosques where he preached with the aim of fomenting disorder when the crowds were dispersing after Gülen's sermons. Due to Gülen's warnings and the already established peaceful practices of the Movement, these attempts failed and the *agents provocateurs* were dealt with by the police.

In 1991, Gülen once again ceased preaching to large mosque congregations. He felt that some people were trying to manipulate or exploit his presence and the presence of Movement participants at these large public gatherings. However, he continued to be active in community life, in teaching small groups and taking part in the collective action of the Movement.

ACTIVITIES, SERVICES AND INSTITUTIONS

46. How does Gülen encourage people to serve humanity?

Gülen encourages people to serve humanity through education and through intercultural and interfaith activities in formal and institutionalized efforts and projects. These services can reduce the gaps between people and nations and establish bridges for the common good and peace. He has explained that society's three greatest enemies are ignorance, poverty and internal schism, which knowledge, work-capital and unity can eliminate.

Ignorance is the most serious problem, and it is defeated through education, which has always been the most important way of serving others. Education is the most effective vehicle for change – regardless of whether it is in Turkey or abroad, and whether or not people have systems working or failing – as the solution to every problem in human life ultimately depends on the initiative and capacities of human beings themselves. Poverty is mitigated through work and the possession of capital, justly deployed in the service of others; and internal schism and separatism are vanquished by striving in forbearance, tolerance and dialogue for unity.

These principles apply equally outside Turkey as within it. The Movement's non-violent and peace-making approach and vision have been widely acknowledged and appreciated.

47. What does Gülen see as the best way to serve humanity?

Gülen argues that because we now live in a global village, the best way to serve humanity is to establish dialogue with other civilizations, to come together on some common ground with mutual understanding and respect, and thus to work for peace, the co-operation of diverse peoples, and the prevention of the predicted clash of civilizations. Gülen has stressed this consistently in his writing: "We can, by coming together, stand up against those misguided souls and skeptics to act as breakers, barriers if you will, against those who wish to see the so-called clash of civilizations become a reality."

48. Which issues do Fethullah Gülen and the Movement address?

Gülen has spoken and written on a wide range of matters – the individual, government, democracy, religion, culture, diversity, integration, alienation, the past and future, tradition and modernity, ethical values, education, tolerance, conflict or co-operation on current events, and more. He speaks and writes about issues such as the analysis of Turkish social structure, religious consciousness and the place and role of Turkey within the international community, and Turkey's right to have a peaceful and constructive say in international affairs.

49. How do Gülen and Hizmet address those issues?

Gülen's style of speech and the way he handles these themes is special. He dwells more on what should be rather than what is. He deals with problems or crises that are plaguing Turkey, not specific people, parties or the State. Gülen discusses these issues in a simple but profound way for the common and greater good.

Hizmet addresses these "hidden" issues in ways that focus collective attention on the critical choices that society needs to discuss and decide, without being ideological. It seeks to educate people through valid projects with flexible strategies.

50. How does Hizmet educate people and contribute to society?

The Movement does not contaminate its cultural and educational purposes with political tactics or political ambitions. Rather than dealing with daily politics, Hizmet makes the latent and dormant power in people visible and makes it assume a shape in terms of educational, health and intercultural and interfaith services and institutions. It expresses issues peacefully and calls for change through taking responsibility and dealing with individuals and their needs, rather than with (or against) political and governmental positions.

As a by-product of the cultural emphasis of its work, Hizmet exposes the contradictions and the silences that the dominant apparatuses of the political system seek to camouflage.

The processes of modernizing institutions and making them proficient and effective have undoubtedly gained in strength through the services provided by Movement participants.

SCHOOLS

51. What is the Movement's chief priority?

The Movement's chief priority is education. In Gülen's view, the lack of well-rounded education hinders the establishment of justice, the recognition of human rights and attitudes of acceptance and tolerance toward others: "If you wish to keep the masses under control, simply starve them in the area of knowledge. They can escape such tyranny only through education. The road to social justice is paved with adequate, universal education; for only this will give people sufficient understanding and tolerance to respect the rights of others."

Gülen holds that a new style of education is necessary. This education will fuse religious and scientific knowledge with morality and spirituality. It will produce genuinely enlightened people with hearts lit by the religious sciences and spirituality, and with minds illumined by the positive sciences. The actions and lives of such people will embody humanity and moral values, and they will understand the socio-economic and political conditions of their time.

The education supported by the Movement is oriented to enabling people to think for themselves, and to be agents of change on behalf of the positive values of social justice, human rights and tolerance. This sharply distinguishes the Movement from exclusivist organizations or cults which are oriented inward and demand conformity from group members. Exclusivist organizations or cults use private rites, insignia, and so on as a badge or indicator of membership, while the Movement has no such attributes.

52. Who responds to Gülen's call to support education?

Gülen particularly urges the social elite, community leaders, industrialists and businessmen to support quality education. Their positive and generous response has enabled the Movement to establish several hundred educational institutions in Turkey and other countries.

53. What kind of schools does Gülen advocate?

The schools inspired by Gülen's educational understanding are not religious or Islamic. Instead, they are secular private schools inspected by state authorities and sponsored by parents and entrepreneurs. They follow secular, state-prescribed curricula and internationally recognized programs.

54. How successful are the schools?

The students and graduates of many of these institutions in Turkey, the Balkans, Europe, Africa, Central Asia and the Far East take top honors in university placement tests and consistently finish at the top in International Science Olympiads. The schools have produced a number of world champions, especially in mathematics, physics, chemistry, and biology.

55. What is Gülen's relationship with the schools in Turkey and abroad?

There is not a single school in the records of the National Education Ministry of Turkey or anywhere else in the world which is registered in the name of Fethullah Gülen; they are all registered in the names of foundations. In Turkey the Ministry of Education carries out the necessary checks in the schools and the hostels in partnership with local authorities. In other countries the schools are all inspected and monitored by the relevant authorities.

When doubts were raised about the effects of the Gülen-inspired schools in Turkey, authorities, scholars and ministers replied that there was no problem in them. Gülen promised that if anyone could show that the schools were teaching anything opposed to modern Turkish and democratic values, he would immediately advise people to close them.

Furthermore, he said that if the Turkish State and authorities would give guarantees on covering the expenses of continuing the education and on keeping the standard of education at those schools at least as high as it is, he would ask that the schools be handed over to the State.

56. Why are they often called "Gülen-schools" if he has no relationship with them?

Because of its brevity, outsiders tend to use "Gülen schools" rather than "Gülen-inspired schools." The shorter term seems to imply some sort of central control of activities and even an ideology, while the second makes it clearer that there is no centralization in the Movement. In fact, as yet there is no consensus among writers on what to call the Gülen-inspired institutions. However, if the term "Gülen schools" is equated with, for example, Montessori schools (where a particular training and qualifications are required for personnel and a specific methodology is used), it is misleading.

Participants have their own perspectives on terms used for the Movement and the social movement organizations (SMOs) participants have set up. However, many outsiders seem oblivious to these perspectives or choose to ignore them. The use of descriptions like "Gülen schools" can arise from ignorance or from attempts to spread disinformation.

Movement participants tend to use the Turkish term *hizmet* (volunteer services) for the projects and services they provide as a whole. This term could be a solution for the inconsistency in naming the Movement and in clarifying the identity of its services and institutions for outside observers.

57. How are the schools financed?

Probably because of its transnational growth since the 1990s, the financing of the Movement is occasionally queried. Some allege that it is impossible for the Movement to have accomplished so much and achieved such rapid expansion without "other financial resources" or some kind of covert funding. However, all academic research on this issue so far has found that each institution and project network in the

Movement is legitimate and transparent in its book-keeping and accounting, and that all financial management is done at the local level and is subject to local inspection. A number of studies of how projects are financed could remove any suspicion of backing by vested political interests.

On this topic insider perspectives also need to be taken into account. Firstly, attitudes to donating time and money to charity vary across cultural traditions. In Islamic and therefore Turkish tradition it is often considered more blessed to give donations anonymously. Onlookers need to be aware of people's sensitivities about such matters. Secondly, in attempting to account for the scale of the Movement's activities in relation to funds available, it is essential to take note of how much of the Movement's resources consist of voluntary, unpaid work, rather than money.

58. Does the Movement dictate the curriculum in the educational institutions?

The Movement does not dictate the curriculum in the schools, universities, and study halls its participants sponsor and manage. The schools have no hidden agenda or targets. The institutions follow national and international curricula and any regulations which apply in the locale where they are established and run. Students are encouraged to use external sources of information, such as the internet and universities' information services.

59. How do the schools convey spirituality and moral values?

For Gülen spirituality includes directly religious teachings, and also ethics, logic, psychological health, and affective openness; so *compassion* and *tolerance* are key terms in his teaching. Gülen believes that non-quantifiable qualities need to be instilled in students alongside training in the exact disciplines. This kind of teaching program is more related to identity and daily life than political action, and it will yield a new spiritual search and moral commitment to a better and more human social life. Those dimensions of education can only be conveyed through example in the teachers' manners, disposition and behavior, not through preaching or direct instruction.

60. Do the institutions outside Turkey have any effect on Turkey's foreign relations?

In the year 2000, in order to give new impetus to Turkey's relations with Central Asian and Caucasian countries, the Turkish Ministry of Foreign Affairs held advisory meetings with Turkey's ambassadors to those countries. The report on the meetings said that Gülen-inspired schools in those countries were having a positive effect on Turkey's relations with their governments.

In a 2003 report prepared for the RAND Corporation, public policy expert Cheryl Benard stated, "Gülen puts forward a version of Islamic modernity that is strongly influenced by Sufism and stresses diversity, tolerance, and non-violence. His writings have inspired a strong multinational following and have proven attractive to young people."

In 2004 Kyrgyz Constitutional Court President Bayekova said, described Gülen as a person of science, peace, and tolerance. Remarking on the international importance of Gülen's work, Bayekova said: "We saw in Gülen an example that, if a person wants, he can achieve as much on his own as a government does. We can establish peace and dialogue if we want. We, as Kyrgyz, work hard to fulfill Gülen's goals."

In 2005 the Romanian commission of UNESCO presented Gülen with an award for his remarkable efforts in activities concerned with dialogue and tolerance and his efforts toward co-operation and peace between the nations of the world.

Turkish diplomatic and even military personnel enroll their children in Gülen-inspired schools abroad, and the reports on the schools by Turkish ambassadors abroad are full of praise. Many other people from all walks of life have also visited the schools and witnessed the quality of education and the positive change in the students and the peoples affected, and expressed their approval. In this way, the schools have also become a means for the Movement to gain recognition.

Also, many Turkish and non-Turkish academics have researched and presented papers about the success and efficacy of the institutions inspired by the Movement at international conferences organized since 2005.

61. Why are some people in Turkey concerned about the schools?

So much positive acknowledgement and recognition outside Turkey of the success of the services, projects and institutions in the Movement has provoked anxiety in the protectionist elite and vested interest groups. These groups prefer to isolate Turkey from world realities, as it is then easier for them to impose their control and authority on Turkish society. These vested interest groups are not recognized for their contribution to any international achievement, but they countermobilize against others who are. Those who countermobilize against Hizmet are simply trying to retain their undeserved status in Turkey and the international arena as the single voice and authority acting on behalf of Turkish people.

The participants and service projects in Hizmet have the capacity to outdo the elite in educational, intellectual, scientific and cultural services and to participate effectively in the international arena. This has revealed the elite's limitations and hurts the elite's standing in the eyes of the people (within Turkey and abroad). The elite finds this an intolerable irritant.

MEDIA

62. How does Gülen communicate his ideas and to whom?

Gülen communicates to a broad cross-section of people through media set up by Movement participants since the early 1980s. He regularly contributes editorials and other writings to several journals and magazines. He has written more than forty books, hundreds of articles, and recorded thousands of audio and video cassettes. Gülen has given speeches and interviews covering many pressing social, cultural, religious, national and international issues. These have then been serialized in different dailies or compiled into books that are best-sellers in Turkey. His writings are available in translation in the major world languages, in print and electronic form through numerous websites.

At the time this book was written, Gülen was in the habit of giving daily or almost daily answers to a wide variety of questions put by those around him and by his visitors. His answers were being recorded and made available freely online in audio and video formats.

63. What specific media organs have Movement participants established ?

Movement participants have established a national and international television station – Samanyolu Televizyonu (STV), a major news agency – Cihan Haber Ajansı (CHA), an independent daily newspaper (*Zaman*) with a daily circulation of over half a million copies nationally, an English-language newspaper (*Today's Zaman*), several leading magazines, and prominent publishing houses such as The Light.

64. In what ways has Zaman newspaper been innovative?

Zaman was established in 1986 and was the first to publish a special US edition in North America. *Zaman* is the only newspaper to print local Turkic language editions all over the Turkic world. It was the first Turkish daily newspaper to make itself available online, which it did in 1995. Special international editions for other foreign countries are printed in local alphabets and languages. The paper is acknowledged for its serious, fair, and balanced reporting. It has won national and international awards for its modern page layout and its contributions to intercultural understanding through its foreign editions.

65. What is the reason for the Movement's interest in the media?

Gülen was the first preacher in Turkey to have his lectures made available on audio and video cassettes to the general public in Turkey. He encourages the use of mass media to inform people about matters of individual and collective concern.

On the qualities of the new type of people who would strive to extend altruistic services to all humanity, Gülen says, "To stay in touch and communicate with people's minds, hearts, and feelings, these new men and women will use the mass media and try to establish a new power balance of justice, love, respect, and equality among people."

In terms of electronic communications and the internet, the Movement was the first Turkish social actor to make itself available online and free to the masses. Since then, through its skills, the autonomy of its language, and the complexity of the strategies that characterize its work, the Movement has been able to influence the debate about the ways in which reality is constructed by the Turkish media. By filtering imposed messages, activating everyday communicative networks, exercising choice among the various media available, and professionally interacting with the media system, Movement participants have themselves become a new medium in the construction of public discourse.

66. How do the media organs contribute to the services and projects?

The media outlets all report on educational and cultural activities as well as news and the perspectives of Movement participants. Thus they are one of the routes by which ideas and good practice diffuse throughout the Movement.

These media outlets have proved to be very effective during times when the values, services and institutions of the Movement were misreported by others. They aim to be visible to the decision-making apparatuses which govern the major media networks and define the political agenda, so that the controversial issues and debates dividing society should not be muffled behind a facade of formal neutrality and self-referentiality.

In addition, they respect and encourage the public discourse which is created in everyday networks by citizens.

DIALOGUE PLATFORMS

67. How are the intercultural and interfaith activities of the Movement viewed in Turkey?

The intercultural and interfaith activities of the Movement are generally seen in a very positive light and as closely related to Turkey's future.

A prominent example of Gülen's personal participation in intercultural affairs (and of the opposition to his work by the protectionist elite) was his meeting with Pope John Paul II. This meeting was seen as a major development. Turkish commentators who criticized Gülen for this meeting were themselves in turn publicly criticized for preferring to be part of an isolationist–totalitarian regime.

So the public and public intellectuals express support for the inter-cultural and inter-religious activities such as the Gülen–Pope meeting. Such activities are seen as a very important security measure for Turkey's democratization and an important contribution toward Turkey becoming a stable country.

68. What are the "Abant platforms" and what is their purpose?

The Journalists and Writers Foundation (JWF) (established in 1994) set up a number of platforms – for example, the Literature, Dialogue Eurasia, Women's and Abant platforms. In common parlance they are all often called the "Abant Platforms", though they are more accurately the "JWF Platforms."

The platforms function as think tanks dealing with contentious social and cultural issues. They bring urgent matters to the fore to be engaged with in a constructive spirit, and start public discussions and negotiations on issues that have caused tensions and clashes for decades. Participants strive to reach a consensus so that diverse views can be peacefully accommodated within society.

These platforms were a pioneering venture in Turkey. At the first meetings of the platforms, those who attended noted that this was the first time in modern Turkish history that scholar-scientists, people of religion, members of the arts, and state officials had come together, sat side by side, and talked and listened to each other with respect.

The platforms have become widely appreciated as an effective forum for airing dilemmas that many people in Turkish society had longed to have openly discussed and resolved. The Movement has thus contributed to the training of a potential for coexistence, for a common sense of citizenship, without the need to clash and with the hope of mutual respect and tolerance.

69. How do the outcomes of the platforms contribute to societal well being?

There has been a tendency in Turkish politics to try to deal with some very complex issues – ethnicity, religious observance, secularism, the role of the military in politics, societal cohesion and peace, work ethics, universal values – in the narrow arena of political competition. However, as a result of this politicization of the issues, hardly any change has occurred in the way that public institutions actually function and operate. The underlying problems therefore continue to perplex the nation.

In contrast to that stagnant situation, the JWF platforms have allowed issues to be aired and to enter the public space so they can be presented to decision making. This transforms the initiatives into possibilities for social change without invalidating the normal decision-making apparatuses of the political arena.

70. What is special about the approach of the JWF Platforms, Fethullah Gülen and Hizmet?

Among the collective actors that take on such problems, the Movement has a marked difference in style and strategy. As it is not a political party and is not trying to gain political power, it does not contaminate its cultural and educational purposes with political tactics or political ambitions. It gives appropriate expression to the issues that need to be addressed, and calls for change through taking responsibility and dealing with individuals and their needs, rather than with (or against) political and governmental positions. In this sense the Movement is able to be more disinterested than a political party or a political movement.

The JWF Platforms generate and disseminate ideas, information, and knowledge. These ideas have a different rationale and permit new words and ideas to be spoken and heard. They are different from the words and ideas that the dominant power groups in Turkey want to impose. This is not to naively ignore the tendency of those dominant groups to assert hegemonic control over political mechanisms and processes; rather, from within the Movement and outside, it is seen as teaching wisely and by example the proper role of social institutions, and as thereby helping to define what participatory democracy in the country could become.

71. How does this generation and dissemination of ideas, information and knowledge help society?

It contributes to an improved level of awareness and understanding of controversial issues. Through media outlets and other institutions as well as the JWF platforms, participants demonstrate their competence to redefine problems and solutions. Intellectuals from a wide spectrum of perspectives are engaged in this effort to improve awareness and to contribute to making sound decisions based on accurate information.

72. How do the JWF platforms differ from other sources of information?

The JWF platforms enable people autonomously to produce and recognize meanings for their own individual and collective lives. This is different from other external and remote powers which manipulate people through the consumption of imposed meanings. The platforms constitute a consensual co-ordination of the plans of action that individuals pursue. They make visible new sources of power and possibilities which can all help to handle systemic conflicts in a complex society. They are new forms of social empowerment and responsibility in Turkey.

73. How successful were Gülen and the JWF platforms in bringing people from different backgrounds together?

Gülen and the JWF platforms succeeded in their aim of bringing different segments of society together for the common good. This was in contrast to those who divide and keep people in their different camps in tense opposition.

People – from left to right politically, from observant Muslims to ardent secularists, from elder statesmen to ordinary citizens, and from ordinary members to leaders of the non-Muslim communities in Turkey – came together in beginning to question the recent past, to see a different reality, and to become open to change and renewal. For example, Armenian Patriarch Mutafian said, "People who shared the same religion could not get together in this country [Turkey] until recent times. Now people from different religions come together at the same dinner. The person to thank for this development is Fethullah Gülen and the Journalists and Writers Foundation of which he is the honorary president. We followed the path opened by him."

74. Have the platforms brought any significant developments or changes in the public space?

Gülen's discourse and practice have obtained the support of many well-known liberal intellectuals and former Marxists. All those people now affirm and accept that the solution to Turkey's problems depends on reaching a consensus. Moreover, some influential scholars, deemed "Islamist" by Western academic circles, have also modified their discourse and action in line with Gülen and express ideas and attitudes different from their earlier positions.

75. Do Fethullah Gülen and Hizmet oppose secularism?

Not at all. As outlined above, Gülen and the JWF have brought together on common ground secularists and anti-secularists, who had been artificially separated on this issue. Gülen argues that secularism should not be an obstacle to religious devoutness, nor should devoutness constitute a danger to secularism. The JWF platforms help to bring these two groups in Turkish society into dialogue.

MOBILIZATION

76. What is a Social Movement Organization?

A Social Movement Organization (SMO) is a formal organization which identifies its goals with the preferences of a social movement and attempts to implement those goals. They may also be called civil society organizations (CSOs).

77. How can the SMOs of Hizmet be categorized?

At the time of writing the SMOs of Hizmet operate in the following fields and categories:

i) Education: pre-school – kindergarten; primary; secondary, high school (normal, science and vocational); higher education – university, language courses, computer courses, university entrance examination preparation courses; study centers for all ages; student dormitories and hostels.
ii) Health: polyclinics, hospitals, health and diagnostic centers.
iii) Media: TV, radio; daily, weekly, quarterly (religious, social, literary, scientific, popular, ecology, children) journals; Writers and Journalists Foundation .
iv) Publishing: publishing houses, printing firms, bookshops, art-design and graphics companies.
v) Business and finance: a bank; an insurance company; an international and other regional business associations; human resources and consultation bureaus; holiday resorts and accommodation.
vi) Humanitarian aid and relief: local/regional, national and transnational aid organizations; reading halls and study centers for the poor and under-privileged; women's clubs and foundations; cultural centers; interfaith dialogue centers.

78. Are the SMOs or services paid services for member-clients?

Of the service organizations listed above, some operate as charity based foundations. All work on the open and competitive market, and some are set up as private companies which are market-oriented. However, they are not commercial enterprises in the sense that they do not privilege market presence and paid services for member-clients; the intention (rather than profit making) is to provide quality services and in this way answer in the best way the needs of people from all walks of life.

79. Are the institutions and SMOs centralized?

In centralized organizations, power resides in a single leader, or a central committee, and local chapters have little autonomy. Hizmet is not organized in that way. The SMOs and institutions in the Movement contribute to the educational, social, and financial well-being of the wider society. Some of them are in formal chains of institutions but not centralized. This decentralization is not a negative reaction to political or administrative centralization. Movement participants do not perceive the existence of any centralized committee or organization and there is therefore no rank–file relationship or discontent with such a committee.

80. How and to whom are the institutions accountable?

There is no community-*versus*-organization or organization-*versus*-community attitude. However, since the various SMOs of the Movement grow and consolidate in widely varying environments, this necessitates division of labor, a variety of different models and specialization in function with more specific definition of roles and norms. Participants in the Movement modify SMOs in secondary details in response to stimuli and limits deriving from peculiarities in the local environment where they operate. However, the SMOs are all accountable to the local authorities (the State) and to their own official inspectors, and comply with the state and international law. This quality of openness, visibility and accountability to the System legitimates the SMOs.

81. Does the Movement have an umbrella organization to co-ordinate a coalition of institutions?

No. Action is not coordinated in that way. Instead, the grassroots participate in the formation of the Movement's culture and contribute to the concrete management of its action by exercising control, by co-ordinating, and by utilizing the information broadcast through the media outlets. Different initiatives may overlap and different individuals may fulfill a number of functions at the same time because they belong to several different and inclusive networks. In most cases, these individuals (rather than institutions) act as informal intermediaries in various forms of inter-organizational relationship. The Movement therefore does not need to have an umbrella organization to co-ordinate or to build a coalition of various SMOs for lobbying or collecting resources.

The other factor which makes an umbrella organization or leadership unnecessary is the degree of cultural development in the Movement. Because of the high degree of cultural development, participant morale is high and so is participants' commitment and tenacity in the face of adversity.

82. Is there any competition between participants, projects and institutions?

Competition between projects and institutions is not restricted. Team work and competition, along with co-operation and consultation between service-projects, are encouraged; competition between individuals is not. Competition is not for self-advancement but is a motivational device to reach for the best and progress within the confines of the social and political order. When it concerns the schools, this can be seen as a competitive struggle for higher profit and better academic results; efficiency based on open competition, both within economic enterprises and educational institutions, is more important than solidarity with cronies or with any specific group of family members, relatives, and/or fellow villagers, etc.

83. How is the division of labor arranged in institutions and service networks of the Movement?

Division of labor is based on formal rules in institutions, while in relational networks tasks are allocated in an informal manner according to the skills that each member is willing to contribute to a project. As formal and institutionalized companies, the SMOs have brought the development of professionalized management in the Movement.

Participants recognize that division of labor, responsibility and managerial authority must be present. Therefore, social and professional control in any SMO is through direct supervision and formal standard rules or universally acknowledged sanctions. This social and professional control is also under constant supervision by the board of directors or trustees related to each SMO. This brings efficacy, the search for satisfactory internal relations and observance of legal boundaries.

84. Does being in an administrative position provide extra, exclusive privileges?

An administrative role does not give anyone greater power or control over strategic resources, nor is it rewarded with significantly greater material advantages. Whether short-term or long-term, an undertaking or project does not provide any justification for any individual to take control of resources of collective action.

85. What is required of those who hold administrative positions in the SMOs? What is required of other participants?

A managerial or administrative role requires greater commitment, liaison and a compatible and holistic relationship with all. However, commitment is regarded not only as a practical day-to-day aim but also a long-term goal for all participants, not just for administrators of the SMOs.

The specialization of the activities of the various individual networks results in division of labor and roles. Participants acquire, develop or consult associative or professionalized expertise. In this way, grassroots and professionalized participants formulate proposals by consensus. The efficacy of projects and institutions is sometimes reported on by the media so that they can be emulated or improved on and obtain useful feedback.

Thus, while the grassroots provide a flow of resources, and the SMOs process and broadcast information and the outcomes, other networks, such as the media, are performing a kind of intermediate representational function.

86. *Why do Movement participants set up institutions?*

Hizmet deals with human needs at the cultural and spiritual level. This provides help and support for individuals against the imposition of lifestyles that do not provide them with the cultural bases for their self-identification. The type of conduct the Movement encourages, and the internal processes of the formation of attitudes do not have political or merely material purposes. The Movement brings collective energies into focus so that deep-seated dilemmas and critical choices can be addressed. It asserts that the individual can only be educated, cared for, and informed within a healthy environment and sound institutions. In order to be able to do this, the Movement sets up new institutions, providing new language, new organizational patterns and new personnel.

87. *What can be learned from the institutionalization of the Movement?*

The institutionalization of the social understanding of Hizmet indicates the great range of its accumulation of knowledge, experience, and expertise. It shows what Hizmet can introduce, innovate and offer to the larger society, humanity and the world. This cultural potential of the Movement is demonstrated in specific issues or specific social fields, and opens up more new arenas for innovation and change.

88. *Why is the institutionalization of Hizmet significant?*

The institutionalization of the services is a success and indicates that people in the Movement have gained new life for their activities via traditional not-for-profit foundations. This helps legitimize the services and institutions and represents an important method of linking society's past and present culture. It is also an important indication of people's need for unity between their culture and modernity. So looking at the institutionalization of societal dynamics in a complex society is a more appropriate measure than simply asking whether or not the Movement is politically effective.

89. *How are the different parts of the Movement connected?*

The institutions and service projects are formally independent of one another; however, they are informed of each other's activities through networks of volunteers and professionals. They all set good examples for one another, and provide alternative perspectives and forums that can be emulated or improved on by others.

The various SMOs which comprise the collective actor of the Movement are autonomous because they work within the limits allowed by the law and the System; they are interdependent because they interact, exchange and benefit from collective outcomes, because they recognize the outcomes as their own, and because the outcomes are recognized as belonging to the Movement and its SMOs by other people and groups.

Because individuals or service-groups are connected by interdependent relationships, any variation in one element has effects on all the others in the Movement. There are mutual relationships which are negotiated, and there are institutionalized relationships which are contractual. Participants and networks use their cumulative experience to adapt, negotiate and devise strategies. They restructure the field of activities in which they are active, and adjust future projects and ways of carrying them out.

90. Is there a covert system of regulations within SMOs of the Movement?

With legal constitutions, SMOs have obvious internal differentiation, functional division of labor, and limits to the area of influence; they work within a limited territory, employ mechanisms of horizontal and vertical co-ordination, and have leadership and personnel selection criteria. They also keep written records. So, except for what is in the legal constitution of each SMO and the law of the country where it is based, there is no other system of laws and regulations that governs procedure or behavior in particular circumstances, or within a particular SMO.

There is no hidden (or informal) disciplinary procedure in any organization. However, in interpersonal social relationships, it is obvious that individuals share their perception of the issues and action. This can have social–moral influence on or implications for individuals in a specific service-network, just as in any day-to-day social relationship anywhere in the world.

91. How do the service networks diffuse themes and experience, and organize circulation of volunteers?

Any service-network may initiate a project or brainstorm around a particular theme. Different service-networks set up committees to study the feasibility of projects without referring to any formal or centralized authority. If a project proves successful, this fact is broadcast or circulated by volunteers, associates in the media or sympathizers in the periphery. The professionalized staffs at other SMOs may then take up issues and take them further. In this way, each SMO represents the collective purpose, but no single SMO can or does claim to be recognized as representing the Movement's collective interests as a whole.

This collaborative framework tends to result in a diffusion of themes and experience, and circulation of volunteers and expertise. It is this commitment to a rich and supportive culture which keeps the SMOs of the Movement viable and continuing.

92. Why is the institutionalization of Hizmet beneficial to wider society?

It is beneficial because formalized SMOs tend to engage in institutionalized tactics. They tend not to initiate disruptive direct-action tactics or use violence to achieve their ends. In the particular case of Hizmet, for the participants the primary loyalty is not to the Movement, or to themselves, but to action, to other human beings and to God; the action is not a temporary instrument but a vocation, even a form of devotion.

93. What facilitated the institutionalization of SMOs?

Prosperity in Turkish society has increased the availability of a wide range of resources. This has facilitated participation in social movements such as Hizmet and its SMOs, as well as the Movement's institutionalization. The projects of the Movement that were formalized or institutionalized in the 1970s are still continuing today, and new ones are always being added.

94. Are the resources of the Movement allocated among the SMOs by a central authority?

No. No single individual in the Movement or in any SMO has the right to distribute power or resources. However, that does not imply that there are no authority structures within SMOs and institutions. The distribution of administrative power can vary within the SMOs, but the local and decentralized control of resources means that resources are not and cannot be reallocated among the collective actors of the Movement by any central authority.

All SMOs in the Movement are formally structured so that resources cannot go unaccounted for or disappear in any way. There has been no evidence to the contrary since the Movement has been around, and the resources referred to are in any case under the control and supervision of the State and legal authorities. This is one of the qualities that make the institutions and their workers trustworthy and commendable in the eyes of ordinary people as well as the authorities.

95. If participants' control of authority and resources is limited, how do individuals manage to carry out their duties?

People in the Movement tend to belong to many networks at the same time and each of these networks will have a greater or lesser number of people in it who take part with different levels of engagement. For this reason, the networks can always find extra workers and volunteers and assign work or tasks to those who are most suited. This also means that a task or a responsibility will be performed by one or more workers or volunteers in one SMO and by others in other SMOs, whether near or far away. While this duplication means that no single person or SMO can gain control of all authority or resources in a particular field, it is also a source of support and collegiality. All this prevents exploitation of the positions, authority and resources assigned to individuals. It provides some kind of inner supervision by all and makes one accountable to all.

The individuals who have assumed projects are continually supervised and supported cognitively, motivationally and, when it is necessary, materially to complete the projects. This provides people with strong incentives, solidarity, cohesion and exchange of experiences among components. Therefore, no one is accused personally of a failure but all marshal the support, direction, consensus and resources necessary for the collective action.

96. If two prospective projects are in the same social field (e.g. health, education, etc.), how do participants choose one project over the other?

Projects are selected for their practicability, legality and effectiveness. They are not exploited for a "politics of signification", that is, in order to gain ascendancy over others or to move up in some existing hierarchy of constituency, class, politics, or credibility; so, projects are not selected for prestige nor for their potential to be attention-grabbing.

There are many reasons why individuals may choose to participate in a particular project; motivational factors arise from the many and varied backgrounds of the participants, the characteristics of the different regions where participants live, work and volunteer, and the formalization and institutionalization of the Movement in over one hundred countries. Thus, individuals perceive their identity and Movement services to be in a high degree of accord within their life space and the world at large. Their own and Hizmet's orientations, interests and values are congruent and complementary. Moreover, as Hizmet's goals and worldview do not depart much from mainstream or pre-existing prospects at hand, participants readily incorporate their energies into the Movement's collective action. Almost a thousand educational and cultural institutions world-wide are considered proof of this.

97. Do service-networks ever select short-term projects?

If specific issues are connected with universal values (peace, human rights, poverty relief, and so on), short-term projects can be taken up, allowing an immediate and correspondingly transitory mobilization. Examples of this have been earthquake relief for Pakistan, Peru and Haiti, Far East tsunami aid, African famine and poverty relief, and other relief efforts in disaster-hit countries.

Such action is carried out within the bounds of transnational consensus and legality. Different components converge in such mobilizations – institutions, the media, luminaries from the art world, and foreign authorities. What is striking about these short-term service-projects is that Hizmet draws especially upon local service-networks, leisure time and also professionalized commitment. In this way, the collective actor of the Movement establishes relationships and co-operates with the institutions or professionalized sectors of the market for short-term mobilizations. A good example of this was the football match organized between a world team and the Turkish national team for Bosnian-Croatian orphans whose education had been disrupted by lack of facilities and finances after the war.

98. Hizmet has significant effects on society so is it not conducting political action, even if it is not party political?

No. Political action and community service are different. Political groups with different political outlooks, worldviews and goals, work for their distinction, separateness and superiority over others. They work self-righteously for positions in a political environment, to be seen and elected. Their separateness and superiority should not be confused with service-networks, which operate altruistically to offer what is lacking in a society, and in which people or groups efface themselves and work without being named or acknowledged. The intention is not to be seen or elected. Quite the contrary, people contribute anonymously.

Compared to political action, Hizmet has a high degree of flexibility in a very adaptable organizational form together with the elasticity of interpersonal relationships. This lets the networks simultaneously fulfill self-reflective functions and produce cultural codes. It enables an easy shift or "bridging" from one function to another. Hizmet's adaptable networks and self-reflective resources support public mobilization and provide the energy for projects. That in turn feeds the networks with new participants, trains new skills and redefines issues and the public space. It is one of the reasons why the Movement has been acknowledged transnationally.

GOALS

99. What questions does Hizmet answer for participants?

Hizmet does not answer participants' questions for them. Instead, in the Movement the participants look for answers to the questions all people living in complex modern societies face. These questions center around how to develop humane qualities, good behavior, love for others, enthusiasm for self-improvement, and an active desire to serve others, make a difference in the world, and to persevere in this desire in the face of setbacks and failures.

The Movement therefore serves as a mediator of demands. It invites and allows society to take responsibility for its own actions within the legal boundaries. It helps to create common public spaces in which people can agree to share the responsibility for a social field. The agreements they make in this way extend beyond party interests or positions.

This kind of cooperation generates innovative energies, keeps the system open, produces innovation and new institutions. It develops elites. It brings into the area of the decidable that which has been excluded. It thus illuminates the problematic areas of complexity in a system. Such a movement is indispensable for the healthy functioning of an open democratic society.

100. What does Gülen believe to be the main problem in the world?

Gülen believes that the main problem in the world is lack of knowledge, and related problems concerning the production and control of knowledge. Producing, maintaining and disseminating knowledge can only be truly achieved through education, but not by party politics. Education is the key to becoming a better, productive and beneficial individual, whether one is Muslim or not. He believes also that the sciences, humanities and religion enhance and complement one another rather than compete and clash. The effectiveness and spread of the Gülen-inspired schools within and outside Turkey are evidence of the success of Gülen's educational philosophy. This philosophy urges personal enlightenment and lays equal stress on the inculcation of ethical values and a sound training in the secular sciences.

101. What did Gülen mean in saying that the true goal of nations must be civilization?

By "civilization" Gülen means a renewal of individuals and society in terms of ethical conduct and mentality. Gülen cultivates a holistic peace through his non-violent lifestyle, the condemnation of terrorism and violence, and his contribution to the mobilization of a movement for spiritual and social change in the world.

Gülen motivates people for purposes other than those imposed by dominant interest groups. He speaks for freedom of speech and consolidation of democratic institutions so that vested interests cannot bend to their own goals the varied values and meanings held by society. He calls for the discussion and redefinition of many social and cultural objects. Accepting the plurality of meanings in the way advocated by Gülen suits the true nature of a civilized human being. His understanding and efforts inspire many to work to find a way out of global crises and conflicts.

102. How can the Movement's goals be characterized?

Firstly, the goals of the Movement are overt. Decisions are made and goals are set in open-to-all service-networks, in the full light of publicity without concealing the existence or objectives of the Movement and without keeping participants' identities secret. Goals are set through rational public discussion and decision making. So the Movement does not establish a separate existence or intention that is free from outside supervision. Another characteristic of goals is that they are consistently positive, constructive and non-disruptive. They are non-violent, non-coercive and peaceful in theory and practice.

In the Gülen-inspired educational institutions specifically, the primary purpose of the education is to ensure respect for objective and universal human values.

103. What goals take priority in Hizmet?

As a result of the diversity of backgrounds of the people in the service-networks, the Movement focuses on general, precise, concrete, unifying and constructive goals rather than changeable and unattainable goals and passing interests. This focus produces within the Movement an understanding of "a permanent hierarchy of interests" in society. The priorities in the Movement are education, interfaith dialogue, and non-political, non-conflictual and non-violent community services, improving oneself and developing social and cultural potential.

The pattern of development, phase and specialization may change in secondary details from country to country. However, the central theme or goal of Hizmet has been never to turn into a political, ideological, oppositional, conflictual or violent movement at any time or in any location. Participants are of course never required, but they are also not allowed, to challenge the constraints established by law or general public norms: the history of the Movement so far has never shown any departure from this principle.

104. Does the Movement share goals with wider society?

Creating alliances, connections and definitions of common goals is central to Hizmet's successes in any of the systems or societies within which participants work. Polls carried out by independent institutions and organizations indicate that the overwhelming majority of the Turkish public and other non-Turkish societies approve of the works and deeds of Gülen and Movement participants. The results of the polls indicate widespread acceptance of the Movement's values and goals.

105. Does the Movement co-operate with other organizations?

Hizmet co-operates with other legitimate and institutionalized organizations concerned with the same issues. It is keen to develop joint initiatives based on compatible definitions. The activities of the educational institutions, such as science and knowledge Olympiads, student exchange programs, the activities of the Foundation of Journalists and Writers all around the world, and local and regional cultural and dialogue centers, and aid-relief work in several countries are good, clear examples of such cooperation.

106. What kinds of goals are not permitted in the Movement?

Political, personal and violent goals are not permitted; action without consensus, that is, any action or initiative taken without any collective reasoning, discussion and consultation is not permitted; personal and material gain by means of services is not permitted; extremism, immorality, and bad habits are not permitted.

107. Are participants in Hizmet fully aware of its goals?

Movement participants have a clear definition of the services, the field of their action, the goals and the instruments used to achieve them. As a result, they know what to expect and what not to expect in return for what they are doing. The Movement also has a great deal of accumulated experience, and it is very successful at imparting this to its participants and to those outside the Movement. The Movement therefore does not experience a gap between unattainable goals and expectations and rewards. Hizmet can be distinguished from direct action, protest movements, cults and sects in a clear way because of its clear general goals and particular objectives, its attainable projects, the legitimacy of the means that it uses and the ends it aspires to, and its accountability about projects.

108. What are the short- and long-term goals of participants in the Movement?

All the short-term goals of participants involve either improving the quality or extending the range of the services offered by the Movement. The long-term goals include self-improvement and earning God's pleasure through such services. Interestingly, some of the short- and long-term goals are the same. For example, participants may aim to improve their own qualifications so as to offer a better service, or to serve a greater number of people. Their goals do not relate only to instrumental objectives, such as seeking social status for themselves or only for a particular community and network, but are more universal in nature. For example, they may wish to spread feelings of love and tolerance, or teach the capacity for dialogue between people who see themselves as different.

109. What makes the Movement universalistic?

It is universalistic because of the type of goals it pursues, the way its institutions and services are managed, the place and weight it gives to socialization, and because it is adaptive and progressive while benefiting from common wisdom. The Movement is also universalistic because it does not seek advantages only for its participants or constituents but strives to benefit society as a whole.

110. Is solidarity an aim of the Movement?

Solidarity is not in itself the cause or primary goal of the formation and the collective action of the Movement. It is a secondary or a tertiary effect which results from the collective services and action. Put simply, the Movement and its participants do not *pursue* solidarity as a goal of their effort; rather solidarity *ensues* from their collective effort. The solidarity which participants experience comes from their doing together what they collectively have approved as a good for themselves and wider society. Such solidarity can be considered a "natural" output (as against "politically contrived" or "artificial" input).

Organizations which pursue solidarity have to attempt to hold people focused inward and "safe" from outside influence or interpretation by the wider public. This contrasts with Hizmet, which always seeks common grounds with others,

111. Are norms and values in Hizmet modified according to changes in circumstances?

No. Varying circumstances do not result in modifications to norms and values in the Movement. Its norms and values have held steady over time, so that the Movement has not suffered or changed as a result of crisis or conflict in society, nor in the face of other new developments, but instead has become stronger. This is different from political movements, in which self-interest and cost–benefit calculations do indeed generally lead to modification of norms.

Hizmet has been able to respond to new developments, the requirements of the contemporary world, and its emergent realities. It has been able to defend or define the meaning of its action with respect to its constant norms and values. So far, no event has provoked any crisis in any area of normative regulation (a change of values) throughout the Movement. Analyzing a collective action such as Hizmet through the lens of self-interest and cost–benefit calculations, or conflicts over allocation of goods in the political market, without referring to symbolic, normative and higher values and meaning, is a reductionist approach. This kind of reductionist approach can reveal little about the Movement. The altruism and personal dedication to valued causes which are visible in the Movement are real and cannot be reduced to self-interest.

112. Do participants enact a variety of political or ideological purposes within or behind the activities or services of the Movement?

No. The goals of the Movement are not focused on building internal solidarity by creating a counterculture. Hizmet is not an ensemble of networks and institutions within which participants can carry on their own activities (public or private), or pursue their own interests (political or commercial). Hizmet is not a means, substitute or subcontractor for some to establish their ideology, politics or economic interests. It is not a parallel society in which a commune or comrade-friends live in an increasingly radicalized way, closed off from the world and global communities. Instead, the Movement is consistent in norms, values and goals. People who support its initiatives but do not identify themselves as "in" it have never complained that its initiatives are based on the ideological or political commitments of the organizers.

113. If the mobilizations are not based on the ideological or political commitments of the participants, why do people take part?

All kinds of people feel that they belong in Hizmet, and through the Movement they find a feeling of belonging to wider society. Their participation starts with short-term projects and objectives. In time this voluntary participation turns into long-term commitment and affiliation, and it becomes the foundation of future altruistic community services. For participants, the meaning of their participation lies in their action, in their voluntary commitment and vocation.

114. How does the Movement overcome the risk of internal conflicts and factionalism?

Hizmet is not an exclusivist and ideological organization or movement. It does not rely on symbolic incentives such as a sacred cause, revolutionary brotherhood, or martyrdom. That kind of reliance increases the risk of internal conflicts and factionalism.

Hizmet does not have a doctrinal orthodoxy, is not an exclusivist organization, and has not suffered any internal disagreement over tactics, goals, or personalities. Also, as the different networks have specific tasks and interests and respond in different ways to the pressing needs of the environment, they do not compete for power. Moreover, as solidarity is not a goal and is not artificially generated, so it cannot be exploited to form factions.

In service-networks there is little significant differentiation of hierarchical roles, and the parameters of projects and rewards for them do not differ a great deal. Furthermore, the tasks which require functional specialization are already carried out by professionalized individuals or networks for the SMOs. People in the Movement co-operate for reasonable, feasible and promising projects which are selected after extensive consultation. So participants do not delude themselves with impractical projects or passing whims. Movement participants have for years tested, proved and learned from their projects, including all kinds of educational efforts and institutions. In the context of the Movement, therefore, groups of participants cannot and do not abruptly break away and launch into uncharted waters.

In short, the processes of consultation, networking and professionalization prevent the emergence of tensions and factions.

115. How likely are fragmentation and schisms?

Fragmentation and schisms are unlikely to form in the Movement for several reasons: Hizmet does not have an ideology; its worldview or belief system is not dogmatically attached to some fixed orthodoxy of interpretation of values and ideals handed on from the past; it is not closed to fresh presentation of its own near reference-tradition (of Islamic scholarship) or to ideas originating outside that tradition; neither is it closed to new formulations and practices that open up a large common source of compatible values and ideals between different traditions.

Gülen and the Movement are not occupied with dogmatic views, but with values such as compromise, stability, protection of the life, honor and dignity of the human being, dialogue and consultation and justice, equity, and human rights. It follows that the Movement's SMOs cannot be demanding a return to the original purity of ideology, or something of that sort.

For its long-sustained positive, constructive and non-confrontational activism, the Movement relies on the social cohesiveness or unity of ideas, means and goals of its diverse participants. It does not rely upon an exclusivist solidarity that separates some of them from others or all of them from wider society and the world. What always matters most is not the numbers of participants but the quality of their inner commitment to the meaning of voluntary, altruistic service as broadly understood within the Movement.

116. Does the choice of projects ever cause internal conflict in the Movement?

Conflicts arise in an organization or a movement because of a) lack of internal communications and co-operation; b) lack of fairness in distribution of resources and incentives; c) deprivation of certain individuals; d) the imposition of unrealistic, unpromising or obsolete perspectives or projects; and e) because of increased personal or collective risks.

In Hizmet, however, participants belong to many social networks as well as taking part in particular service-projects. Also, participants have access to mass communication about the activities and values of the Movement through the media and press organs. The Movement, therefore, does not lack resources for communication. It does not lack opportunities to pursue different but complementary strategies. It is able to provide its participants with new explanations or perspectives for any emergent realities.

The localization of projects and collective decision making prevent feelings of unfairness about resources and incentives, thwart the imposition of unrealistic or obsolete projects, and avert any potential risk taking. For all these reasons, internal conflicts become unlikely in Hizmet.

117. Is the Movement hiding its intentions?

No. The Movement does not envisage or intend an overall, sudden change in people and/or in the direction of the development of projects. The intention is to educate people with patience and dedication over time in order to enable them, in peace, to manage the complexity and plurality they have to deal with.

Decision making in service-networks is neither centralized nor invisible. Project development decisions are not taken by specific individuals or private groups. As people are allowed to intervene in the decision making, the process is participatory, and the existence of concealed intent to make sudden changes is not feasible or credible.

118. Does the Movement claim it brings transformation in larger issues?

No. Hizmet does not advance an unrealistic claim to deliver overall transformation in systemic or global issues. However, its collective action responds and offers workable solutions to the local problems and issues which arise from systemic inefficiencies and global concerns. The self-reflexive capacity, competence and efficiency of the Movement give it the potential to address and tackle the problems of modernity. The Movement helps to formulate solutions at the level of individual autonomy. This potential and autonomy prepare individuals for peaceful development and healthy integration into the contemporary era.

Contemporary societies are complex and change in them can only be managed by education, information, interaction and co-operation. Very little, if anything at all, can be achieved by unilateral action, coercive application of force and the wasting of human life either by bloodshed in war or by economic strangulation. Beneficial and sustainable change entails decisions, choices, accord and co-operation within and between societies and civilizations. In this way only consensually valued projects and policies are achieved. Person by person, project by project, the Movement is working towards beneficial and sustainable change.

119. In what way does the world "need" a movement like Hizmet?

The circumstances in which we live today necessitate a far better educated, fairer and more peaceful world and the co-operation of civilizations. Hizmet makes continual investment and conducts a continual search for individual and institutional improvement and development. It works by consensual decision making, rotation of chairmanships in managerial positions, and supervision and inspection of SMOs by boards. It pays due attention to expertise and good counsel. Its participants come together to build and maintain effective and efficient SMOs that meet local needs in many different societies worldwide.

The world seems likely to continue to need human efforts like those of Hizmet. Gülen's thought, which inspires the work of the Movement, offers intellectual and spiritual resources that help people to meet the challenges of living in the modern world.

PARTICIPATION, IDENTITY AND THE INDIVIDUAL

120. What kind of people participate in Hizmet and why?

Many people from all walks of life and different intellectual backgrounds participate in the service projects. The types of service Gülen advocates – education, health, intercultural and interfaith dialogue, cooperation of civilizations – require action, and concern relationships in the everyday lives of all members of society and humanity.

121. What is the nature of relationships in the Movement?

The relationships are *affective*–interpersonal, social, informal and integrative; *professional* – formal and contractual; *cultural* – educational, self-reflective, altruistic and apolitical; *locational* – project-based and inclusive; and *transnational* – peaceful, collaborative and civilizing.

122. What attracts participants to working and volunteering with Hizmet?

People are attracted to Hizmet by reading Gülen's works and listening to his lectures, by the overall meaning and the message of the altruistic services, and by the worldview of the Movement. They may have exemplary friends from the Movement or know Movement participants in their immediate environment, among their neighbors, and relatives, and they are attracted by their conduct and sincerity.

123. What are the basic attributes of Movement participants?

They are very aware of what they are thinking and doing, fully integrated and dedicated to their jobs, and willing to sacrifice much in their personal lives for the service, including leaving home to work abroad.

124. What social backgrounds do people in the Movement come from?

The overwhelming majority of participants are young university students. The next largest group (almost as numerous) consists of university graduates. The average age in the Movement is 25–30. Most of the students or people in the service-networks are middle or upper-middle class. They are from better integrated backgrounds, urban, with a high level of academic achievement.

The volunteer–participants are in the main from the educated and urban middle class, relatively privileged and better integrated: they hold the technical and cultural competence or an economic-functional position that makes them more likely to mobilize because they see the contradictions of the system, and their educational level and intellectual milieu foster egalitarian and anti-authoritarian values.

125. Has participation by university students radicalized the Movement?

No. Participation among university students and educated newcomers from a wide variety of social experiences and backgrounds has grown, but this has not radicalized the Movement, nor caused cleavages to emerge either in it or Turkish society. The participants in fact prioritize individual achievement in private, expansion of freedom of expression, and democratic participation.

126. What is the influence of people who join the networks in the Movement at a later stage in their lives and have previous affiliations to other movements?

They come into the Movement because they would like to be part of a system which is already working. The Movement makes available venues and channels to express opinions, convince people and come to a majority decision. New participants with previous affiliations can, of course, access these channels. However, perspectives which are not in accord with the general principles of the collective action of the Movement may be aired but cannot be imposed on the majority. So newcomers to networks often orient themselves towards new goals of transformation.

Unless participants acknowledge and disseminate the worldview of Hizmet, and contribute in some way to the services, they will find it difficult to be recognized as taking part in the Movement.

Integrating with a service-network or institution, however, does not require them to forsake other social networks to which they belong, but they can utilize them to circulate the new messages and meanings that they learn.

127. What is the nature of membership of Hizmet?

There is no formal membership as such in the Movement. Individuals do not belong to any single community or network only. What distinguishes Hizmet is the multiplicity of its participants' affiliations; they participate simultaneously in a number of areas of social life and in associations of various kinds.

Author and journalist Abdullah Aymaz exemplifies these multiple affiliations: "I am a teacher and a writer. I have commitments like my job and also voluntary extra contributions at the media organ I work for as a columnist. I also take part in neighborhood and community work where my family resides. I have interests in scientific issues and therefore take part in the editorial board and the selection committee of a popular scientific monthly. My children attend a high school and I take part in the family group of the school to improve the educational level of the school. I also engage in interfaith dialogue and visit and receive people from different faith communities. I also attend meetings and networks of people from my own hometown and former places I lived in. In short, I participate in several networks due to my place of residence, job, interests, hometown, children's education, and so forth. Likewise, there are thousands of people attending more networks and doing more community services in the Movement than I do."

In each of these settings only a part of the self, and only certain dimensions of the personality and experience, are activated. In a religiously motivated search, alternative affiliations are a journey for personal and spiritual development and meaning.

128. Are participants drawn from people on the margins of society?

Neither newcomers nor existing participants are unintegrated, excluded, marginal or rootless people. Research shows that participants are people who are active and integrated into the community. This contradicts the common supposition that mobilization is a phenomenon involving those who are most affected by social disintegration and exclusion. In fact, availability for mobilization is weak among such marginal and rootless groups. Those who become participants in a movement generally have a more solid collective identity and closer ties to a network of social affiliations.

The individuals who form the service-networks in the Movement include a very high percentage of people from a middle-class or higher socio-economic position. They develop a broader vision of the world. They become sensitive to particular and global concerns and causes. They acquire information and necessary skills and competencies to deliver service-projects that meet real social needs.

Participants very openly engage in projects for education, culture, interfaith dialogue, societal peace and civilizational co-operation. This brings them recognition as bearers of universal ethical values, not ideas or orientations that are narrow, marginal or exclusive.

129. What is the socio-economic background of those who do not belong to the Movement but support its collective action?

They are highly diverse and widespread. It is difficult to identify specific social categories within the varied socio-economic groups that maintain a co-operative (but not participatory) relationship with Hizmet. They belong to an increasing number of roles and professions.

However, it is possible to say that the overwhelming majority of educated participants in the Movement do not work in religiously oriented occupations but in education, engineering, the sciences and business. They support a moderate faith-inspired initiative to build a network of schools, universities, hospitals, media and businesses. This is interpreted as a "third way" between the forces of militant secularism and radical Islamism. That too is a factor encouraging more co-operative support for the Movement from non-participants or "third parties." Good examples of such people can be found in the book, *Barış Köprüleri: Dünyaya Açılan Türk Okulları* ("Bridges of Peace: Turkish Schools Opening to the World"), a compilation of twenty-seven articles written by "third-party" statesmen, politicians, scholars, thinkers and journalists. The articles discuss more than 300 educational institutions and other efforts of Hizmet volunteers in ninety countries.

130. What makes people decide to join and contribute to service networks?

Individuals perform the greatest role in the process of becoming involved in the Movement. Prior interpersonal contact is the single richest source of Movement volunteers. Relationships through social life facilitate involvement and make it easy and comfortable for individuals to join and contribute to networks of services.

Within these networks, individuals interact and engage in negotiations as they develop the frameworks of ideas and motivation that are necessary for action. People by their free will accept roles that are in accord with their individual differences and personality traits. Individuals come into these service groups with a conscious decision to change and to direct their own existence.

In these social contexts, people can discuss appropriate action and activate material resources, cultural capital and labor. The social and cognitive processes in such contexts help develop a rationale that legitimates a project's formation and any follow-up projects. In addition to the rationale, people also develop a belief that the project or institution and its services are truly necessary and worth all contributions that they make.

131. How do participants become integrated into service projects and networks?

As there is not a single dimension to human behavior, all problems are first brought for solution to networks of people, into the communicative process. At the same time individuals become informed within the collectivity. Then they voluntarily integrate into relational networks of educational, social, and altruistic services. Hizmet does not give identity to people, but provides resources for them to construct their own identity. It makes them responsible for both that identity and their action.

132. What is the cost for the individual of entry to and exit from the Movement?

The low or zero cost of entry into and exit from project-networks means that participation can be temporary and short-term. It does not demand denial or rejection of the participants' other affiliations, relationships or worldviews. Participation in a specific project might be short-term but an individual's commitment to values and meaning in the collective action of the Movement is not. Individuals rarely go out of the Movement but offer to participate in another project. This ability to move from one project or institution to another is not hindered by the project-networks in the Movement if a participant wishes it.

The great number of other projects and networks available makes it easy for the individual to move into another service-network or project. The sharing of short-term goals means that only one segment of individual experience is placed at stake. In this way, individuals or groups of people in any service-network do not develop any false assumptions of individual failure, exit or betrayal.

133. How does moving from one service-network to another affect participants?

The plurality of goals and resources in the Movement means that individuals can change networks with only minor consequences for the improvement and effectiveness of either their contribution or the network. In addition, as the range of possible service-networks of choice is expanding with the increase in the range of roles and activities in the Movement, leaving one group for another becomes less dramatic an event for the individual.

Individuals do not join the service-networks on an individual basis alone, nor act or work in them out of self-interest. They do so through relational channels, such as friends, neighbors and professional associations. Individuals have the opportunity in service-networks to come to know one another as human beings. This informal fellowship develops a common sympathy which contributes to intimacy and social cohesion or solidarity. The Movement therefore does not need any formal ceremonial behavior, ritual, symbols, slogans, costumes or badges to foster identity or unity. Newcomers keep their relations with other people who are outside the Movement. They are not encouraged to drop or neglect anybody.

Participation in the Movement is based on information-sharing, exchange and interaction and on taking an active role in the collective action. It takes the form of friendship-based circles. It is contextualized: people in it have simultaneous and multiple interests and friendships, and professionalized and altruistic commitments. Losses that may arise for any reason are therefore not borne by the individual in loneliness or isolation.

134. Do people join networks in the Movement because they lack other options?

No. Being part of a network in Hizmet is not due to lack of choice but out of free choice. It is by conscious decision that individuals become part of the Movement and then enact and experience self-fulfillment in it. Therefore, the collective action of the Movement proves for many to be a call or vocation. Moreover, in the various service networks in which they participate, people are further motivated and inspired by the ideas and tactics of other participants.

135. Why is it important that participation in the Movement is voluntary?

Individuals freely join associations and services of their choice, and they are also free to exit, without cost. Whether the underlying motivation for such voluntary participation is self-fulfillment, self-expression, self-development or something else, it expresses the individualistic nature and aspect of civil society.

136. Is the Movement trying to build a separate, exclusive society?

The majority of people who participate in the services are introduced by friends. The fact that it is not via relatives or through some kind of clan system shows that relationships in the Movement can be inclusive, transformative and lasting. Also, the fact that introduction to and participation in the Movement or service-projects occurs through acquaintances in everyday life and through work colleagues indicates that the cultural perspective or worldview of Hizmet is regarded as legitimate and rational. The participation of individuals who did not grow up within an associated community or its networks is also significant: it indicates purely individual choices and a strong subjective identification; people make an active rationalizing and reckoning of the decision to participate in the collective action of the Movement.

137. How are participants in the Movement able to establish and retain their links with the wider public?

The dense, strong and multiple affiliations that individuals enjoy within project-networks inspire, motivate and commit them to the services the project yields. But participants do not separate their private lives from those projects. Rather, they link their private lives to their public activities and their societal environment. This leads to harmonious and peaceful continuities rather than detachment, alienation, frustration and antagonism.

There are also a great number of individuals who are sympathetic to the collective action of Hizmet but do not become active in it. This indicates that the Movement is not an isolated actor and is able to establish affective links with and among the wider public. Indeed, there is no expectation in the Movement that participants should sever previous social ties. They are expected to have other ties too, and to make new ties while "in" the Movement. Such multiple affiliations are in principle and practice welcomed: loyalty centers upon effective delivery of service-projects and complementarity between them. It does not center upon the Movement as such. Solidarity among participants ensues from sharing work effort and from shared experiences and memories; it is not pursued as a precondition of doing the work at all.

138. In what way are the Movement's networks beneficial to wider society?

Hizmet has been mainly organized through informal, everyday life cutting across interpersonal relationships. This links the participants of local communities to each other. Within these networks relationships are embedded in systems of relationships based on friendship, neighborhood, professions, and personal interests. Relationships range through social, cultural and religious, communitarian and humanitarian activities. The activities exceed by far the sphere of overt political activities and link across localities and generations. Participants have proven themselves capable of bridging ideological and social barriers through multiple participations, and capable of strengthening mutual trust.

Although they seem relatively simple, the networks play a significant counseling role that connects individuals to broader social dynamics and diverse SMOs. New potentials in the society that that might be drawn to conflict and violence are thus transformed into productive, collective and useful actions and constructive projects.

139. Why is Hizmet made up of service-networks?

Hizmet exhibits a unified identity based upon beneficial services for all, and is organized in networks because the relationships in the Movement are not hierarchical, mechanical or predetermined. This way, one group or network does not impose on others a greater burden of limitations or liabilities. The networks allow a relationship of autonomy and interdependence

Researchers in sociology have measured self-efficacy and find that the more active movement participants are, the more assertive, self-confident, energetic, and effective they are in using their capabilities, as compared to those who are less engaged in activism.

In everyday life, intimate interpersonal relations and emotional relationships with those closest to them allow individuals to make sense of their world through networks. Interpersonal interactions and affective bonds are the fundamental background to movement participation. Through the service-networks people become more able to reach out to other systems, relations, meanings, goals and interests. Without such networks, it is not possible for most people to reach out to all these on their own.

140. How do individuals and groups in the Movement "make sense of their world through networks"?

Individuals and groups have come together in the Movement to make sense of their being in togetherness and in action. They recognize and sustain the meanings, values and plurality of aspects that they find in being and acting together. They share orientations that bind actors and the specific way of acting together through time. They share, within the opportunities and constraints, what is produced by their work. They share also the definitions of legitimate goals and ways of achieving them, the field in which they are working, and what sort of investments they can make in a project and what rewards they can expect. These continuous processes become a network of active relationships between actors who interact, communicate, influence each other, negotiate, and make decisions.

141. Does all the shared work by participants in the Movement make it a rather exclusive group?

In fact, people can participate in the service-projects and institutions of the Movement at various levels of commitment and with different degrees of involvement. To be sure, a shared identity characterizes the Movement as a whole. But different levels of affiliation of participants and non-participants with the service-projects and SMOs make the identity of Hizmet open and inclusive.

Networking, participation and affiliation within the Movement are not alienating or sectarian because the Movement is open to the outside world, and it does not have or seek a totalitarian organizational structure but instead has and seeks compatibility with other collective actors and civil society bodies. Hizmet is not restricted to a certain time and place (or territory). However, this inclusiveness has no negative effect on the homogeneity or effectiveness of the service-projects.

142. Don't participants have to give up many things and devote their lives to Hizmet?

There is no such obligation on participants. Individual commitment to a specific project or a specific service-network does not demand a life-term involvement. Individuals pass from one service-network to another, and involvement may be temporary.

Participants in the Movement belong to many social networks and enjoy the full complexity of human relationships. This permits individuals to look for and take up practical opportunities for the self-planned integration of personal experience in everyday life. Self-fulfillment is through self-willed formation of meaning, and self-planned integration and experience.

143. Do the relational networks function as a substitute for family or other relationships?

No, the relational networks do not take that kind of form. Instead, they are built and strengthened through interaction and through the value that is attributed to individual views, to contribution to philanthropic projects and to collective reasoning. Individuals are not looking for a communal identity, or to replace or relocate primary associations (gender, age-group, locality, ethnicity, etc.). The participants are not previously isolated people. They do not see the Movement as a surrogate family. They are not using networks as a temporary means to search for identity or to achieve or resist political power. They find an authentic relation to themselves and to others and therefore call one another and the whole society to responsibility.

144. Why do participants stay in the Movement even after leaving an institution or finishing a service-project?

At the moment of joining the service-networks, individuals might not bring a profound personal investment. Rather, their commitment and contribution increase as their knowledge of the field in which they have come to contribute grows and matures. This investment progressively strengthens the participant's bond with a service-network or SMO, and is a cultural investment.

Relationships constructed in this way are far deeper and more binding than short-term participation, and they outlive short-term participation. They are completely unlike participation in actions and organizations with totalizing accents (i.e., with extreme and oversimplified definitions of people and of the field of action). The capacity that participants develop in networks to reflect on themselves and on the action and their direct participation in the collective action makes their experience make sense for them. The cultural, symbolic and plural form of the service-projects in the Movement respects individual differences and needs.

145. Why do Gülen and the Movement lay such emphasis on collective effort in service-networks?

Within these networks of services people come to understand that the vast potential to make a change in the lives of others is far broader than their own actual individual capacity for action. Through the establishment of social relationships, people become open to the personal realization that an individual is limited and not even sufficient unto himself or herself. On the other hand, they have opportunities to compensate for their limitations in community service through the potential of the collective actor.

146. How is this integration into the service-networks different from susceptibility and submission to the authoritarianism of some political movements?

The majority of participants in Hizmet are already educated and come from positively acknowledged backgrounds. They are not misguided or inadequate individuals. They are not beguiled by a utopia, an authoritarian coercive leader, or by any attempt at defying authority to bring a regime change in Turkey.

The participants join the networks with the resolve that they can do something helpful for society and it can really work. The intention is altruistic rather than selfish; they are not trying to change the direction of the development of the System.

Furthermore, neither psychological nor political situational stress is the only necessary reason for joining a movement, and such stresses are not reflected in the patterns of participation in Hizmet.

147. Have there been any instances or accusations of coercion, punishment or duress in the Movement?

There is certainly no pressure to join, believe or conform in the Movement. All participants are voluntarily and consciously involved. There have been no instances or accusations of coercive persuasion, manipulation of consciousness, forced self- or ego-destruction, brainwashing or psychological punishment or duress. None of these account for people taking part in the Movement.

Belonging to a community-based project or a service-network in the Movement signifies the integration of an individual into a collective where there are appropriate channels for the expression of people's aspirations and intentions to serve humanity. Moreover, participation is open-ended and multiple. People take part in intersecting and overlapping networks of affiliation. The service-networks can communicate with one another. At the same time each can be internally integrated but externally separated from the others by geography, objectives, local realities or regional sensitivities. Individual mobility and multiplicity of affiliations are encouraged and available to all in the Movement. Associative, occupational, communal and institutional channels to handle demands are always open and help to prevent segregation and conflict.

148. If people can enter and exit at will, how is the question of the "free-rider" handled in the Movement?

"Free-riders" in a social movement are those who do not get actively involved if they think that it is risky or costly to them; they leave activism to others, yet take a share of any good or benefit achieved. The potential negative effects of this kind of "free-rider" attitude are limited by internal factors of the Movement, such as the participants' choice of projects, self-fulfillment, altruism and vocation. In addition, face-to-face discussions, availability of information and communication channels, skilled leadership in SMOs, and self-willed choice of a network and freedom to exit or withdraw from service-networks in the Movement obstruct the development of the "free-rider" problem in the first place.

In faith-inspired service-projects, expectation of reward from God alone, the purity of intention, or the accountability to God for one's deeds and intentions, which may all be called piety or God-consciousness, help prevent, or at least minimize, this problem.

149. How is identity gained or given in Hizmet?

For Hizmet identity is not something imposed by belonging and membership in a group; it is constructed by the individual in her or his capacity as a social actor. It is always in accord with social capacity. A feeling of relationship is formed at the level of the single individual, and awakens the enthusiasm and capacity of the individual for action. Through sociability people rediscover the self and the meaning of life.

The altruistic service urged by the Movement is this effort of human sociability and relationship. Therein lies the core of the distinctiveness of the Movement. It does not lead to a flight into a myth of identity. It does not draw an individual into an escapist illusion so that he or she is magically freed from the constraints of social action or behavior. It reaffirms the meaning of social action as the capacity for consciously produced human existence and relationships.

150. So where do participants feelings of identity come from?

Identity in Hizmet is not taken as something given. It is dynamic and always the result of an active process and has continuity. Since the participants willingly take on, own and retain it, their identity is not imposed. The real-world-oriented social service and project networks in the Movement cannot impose any kind of identity on participants. Individuals construct their identities through their deeds, action and services, intention and goals in the Movement, and their personal choices and character.

151. How do people recognize one another as part of the same movement?

The relationships, services and their outcomes give a sense to participants of being a "we", and sustain an unspoken solidarity among projects and the goals that their institutions pursue. This yields reciprocal recognition of the identity of the Movement as collective actor.

152. Is there any risk of participants losing their individuality in service-networks?

No, this risk does not arise because individuals themselves construct the multiple social relationships of their everyday life. They can easily adapt themselves to projects for the betterment of the conditions they live in. They can thus build direction and meaning for their existence in relational and professionalized networks and services.

Individuals do not run any risk of losing themselves in the service-networks. They feel that their individual differences are respected. They do not cease to exist as unique and singular individuals but come to appreciate the network connections between people. Their interaction and communication, the basic requirements of social life, are more easily maintained and mediated by networks of belongings. Through these networks, people orient themselves toward living at peace with the Movement and with the outside, wider public.

153. By what means does Hizmet influence the lives of individuals, the community and society?

The private initiatives and competitiveness which the Movement encourages in support of public and philanthropic services are all based on free choice. They are grounded on voluntary participation and occur simultaneously at several levels of the social space and system. The Movement has assumed a bottom–up approach to transforming individuals through education, communication and co-operation, rather than the top–down approach that is typical of a government, state or regime which is attempting to bring about a change.

So, the Movement has not mobilized to claim a different distribution of roles, rewards and resources, nor clashed with the authorities and power. Participants are not using educational and intercultural efforts as instruments to push the limits of the system. They wish, while holding on to their identity and moral values, to be a modern partner and contributor to the European and wider global community.

154. If Hizmet is not centralized or authoritarian, how does it achieve cohesion?

Participation in services takes relatively stable, enduring forms. Individuals come and go and replace one another but the projects remain and continue. Individual needs and collective goals are not mutually exclusive; they are one and the same thing, and in daily life coincide and interweave closely with the action of the Movement. The Movement thus becomes a vehicle, a means, for people to transform latent potential into visible collective action. Participation in services around a specific goal and the tangibility of the products yield and strengthen solidarity. Externally visible aspects of the mobilization, and its rapidity, extension, and success, reflect the inner solidarity of the participants.

The social cohesion in the Movement is cultural in character. To a certain degree, the solidarity of the group is inseparable from the personal quest and from the everyday affective and communicative needs of the participants in the network. Yet it remains incidental to the main aim, not a goal pursued for itself; rather, it accompanies action naturally as a result of experiences and memories gained, and it is retained through the labor of accomplishing collective projects.

155. How can the apparent unity in the Movement be explained?

Hizmet is oriented toward action and goals. This orientation builds in the Movement a fairly cohesive and homogeneous identity. It strengthens the face-to-face human and psychological interaction and, in turn, facilitates collective action of all kinds, including SMOs. Many collective actions have different orientations, components and levels relating to different socio-historical levels or layers in a given society. The collective actor of the Movement too identifies and recognizes specific levels and a plurality of levels within the construction of collective action and identity. However, it does not negate and attempt to eliminate people's differences, but tries to bring them around mutually acknowledged similarities and references so that they can serve their communities and humanity. It does not focus on secondary, contradictory and ambivalent differences which have little significance for universally accepted projects, such as education. So the message of the Movement carries a complex articulation of meanings, relations and values for peaceful coexistence and co-operation of civilizations. Hence, to reduce the Movement to just one of its many levels, to conflate all these elements into the unity rendered by ideologists or into only the dimensions of collective action that are visible at first sight, is either an error or reduction.

156. Doesn't distinguishing itself from the environment lead the Movement into conflicts?

Hizmet has learned to distinguish itself from the environment without leading to isolation from it or conflict. It does not cut itself off from society. It is the relational dimension of the collective identity of Hizmet that helps to form unity within the collective actor, not any attempt to remain distinct from the surrounding society.

The Movement as collective actor is able to recognize the effects of its action and meanings. It attributes these effects to itself and exchanges them with others. Because of the effects of its action and meanings, the Movement is able to establish relationship, links and bonds through services with the wider public. This also facilitates the solidarity that binds individuals to each other; this auto-identification and differentiation of the actor from others then brings about the exchange of social and mutual recognition with other collective actors.

157. Does the Movement engage in identity politics (based on faith or nationality, for example)?

Hizmet does not engage in identity politics. It does not seek to be different from other people, ethno-religiously, culturally or geographically. The Movement sees a radical form of identity politics as dangerous for society because of its intolerance, exclusivism, and self-defeating fundamentalism.

Movement participants accept and abide by Turkish and international norms, regulations and laws. They share the concerns and problems common to people all over the world, and work to contribute to their resolution. The worldview, intentions and efforts of the Movement are accepted and approved by the overwhelming majority of people in Turkey and by those who know their efforts outside Turkey. So the Movement is able to become an agent of reconciliation between diverse communities around the world. These efforts are put into practice through legal, formalized and institutionalized means.

The Movement is defined in terms of its social and multicultural relations; its intention to seek consensus among communities legitimates its transnational projects, so that it does not deviate into, or let others be led astray into, fundamentalism and sectarianism.

158. How can Hizmet adapt to the environment while maintaining its own identity?

The Movement's ability to maintain its identity compared with its variations over time and establishment of new relationships, organizational forms and institutions, and adaptations to the environment can at first appear contradictory: while the Movement tacitly affirms its difference from the rest of the society, it also states its belonging to the shared culture of society and its need to be recognized as a social actor for the common good. This seeming paradox is in fact a necessary prerequisite of a multicultural, diverse and pluralist society and presupposes a certain equality, a degree of reciprocity, and consolidation of democratic practice and institutions.

Movement participants feel a bond with others because they share the same interests. This enables individuals in the Movement to make sense of what they are doing. It enables them to affirm themselves as subjects of their action, and to help to prevent the breakdown of social relations during conflicts.

159. How can the Movement be autonomous without being alienated?

The Movement has shown that it can maintain a stable, durable self-definition over many years. Indeed it has improved its ability to resolve problems that are posed by the environment. It is becoming increasingly autonomous in its capacity for action within the network of relationships in which it is situated.

The *February 28 Process* also proved that the Movement has the ability to produce new definitions and meanings by integrating the past with the emerging elements and outcomes of a present situation into its stable identity. This in turn strengthens its internal cohesion and locates common ground outside itself. Therefore, while the methods and means to accomplish services may change or develop over time, the core of the identity in the Movement does not change with time and situation: it holds steady.

Furthermore, the strong support for Gülen and the activities of the Movement (especially during the defamation period following the *post-modern coup*) from a very wide spectrum of politicians, statesmen, civil society organizations and journalists corroborates the idea that the identity of the Movement is integrative rather than alienated.

160. How do participants react to accusations that they are sectarian, fundamentalist, reactionary, etc.?

The participants do not respond to such accusations with direct action. Instead, they turn their attention from rhetoric to the visible realities and concrete results of the Movement's collective action; they look to education and to useful, beneficial, altruistic community services and peace. Movement participants tend to differentiate themselves from political action; their cultural level marks them off from all others, especially from sects or cults.

161. What elements shape the identity of the Movement?

The collective identity of the Movement depends on the way that a multitude of choices, goals, relations, services and representations are held together. It is the outcome of conscious, laborious processes. However, some dimensions of a social movement's collective identity may be weaker or stronger than others, and some may have secondary or tertiary priority. In the case of Hizmet, some (such as political power or governmental change) do not even make it into the classification.

The identity of Hizmet is not shaped by transcendent, metaphysical and meta-social elements and entities, such as myths, legendary saints, idealized ancestors or sacral celebration of any individual. On the contrary, although the Movement is a faith-inspired initiative and the founding elements come from Islam and its universal values, it increasingly and progressively associates itself with purposive human action, culture, communication and social relations resulting from the services it provides.

Because of feedback – criticism and praise – from outside the Movement, the collective identity is the product of conscious action, the outcome of self-reflection, and more than a set of given or "structural" characteristics. The Movement is becoming increasingly self-reflexive, inclusive, integrative and universalistic due to its conscious collective construction of identity within a widening transnational environment of social relations.

162. What maintains the collective identity and action of Hizmet over time?

Its collective identity is constructed through a combination of rational exchange, affective connections and bonds, mutual recognition, purposive calculation and meaningful action. Participants' personal choices, meaning, emotion, and expectations and interactions are all measured against the collective actor's field of operation and reality. This assessment comes from the possibilities and limits of action, which help the collective actor to define itself, its environment and relationship with that environment.

The maintenance of the identity of the Movement is also a collective interactive process because many individuals or networks play a role in defining the meaning of their action. Many take part in maintaining their ongoing relationships with other individuals and groups, and in calculating the field of opportunities, constraints, costs and benefits for any action. So the Movement's identity needs to be treated at both the individual and collective levels because human beings create their identities through relationships, not only by what separates them from others, but by their many links with the people and the environment that surround them.

Consequently, people make social, cultural, cognitive and emotional investments in the inter-relational networks in the Movement. Through these, individuals feel part of a common unity, a social coherence and cohesion. Because people interact and because they exchange ideas and convey them to others through social relationships, they can rationalize, discuss, define and defend their relationships. It is this interaction and communication that maintain the collective identity and action of the Movement over time.

When a collective actor proves able to handle assaults and countermobilization cognitively and intellectually, while remaining within the limits of the System, and while remaining unaffected by environmental and conjunctural changes, the actor or the identity has gained a certain stability and permanence. The collective actor then starts to be easily recognized by friends, opponents and third parties. The ability to recognize and to be recognized over time distinguishes the Movement from other collective actors and highlights its potentiality.

This collective and continuous process is manifested in forms of organization, internal rules and procedures, and professionalized leadership relationships, all of which feedback and crystallize the identity of the Movement.

163. How has the Movement become a set of cultural referents and a life model for so many people?

As a result of wise, flexible guidance, awareness of the proper and efficient means for the achievement of particular objectives and general goals, and prudent concern for the lawfulness or legality of both means and ends, the social and cultural practice of the Movement has gained participants from all social categories and most age groups in different parts of the world. The fact that Hizmet is related to the world in a global interaction turns it into a set of cultural referents and a life model.

REWARDS AND INCENTIVES

164. What does the Movement offer its participants?

It offers an opportunity for individuals to construct meaning for themselves by unselfishly doing some good in their own environment and for people around them. It enables them to do this without contention or violence. They do not need to seek to disadvantage any person or institution or to diminish their power or question the legitimacy of their authority to exercise that power.

165. In the Movement, where do rewards come from?

The rewards to be expected as a result of services provided are strictly from God. The Movement does not offer selective incentives (atomized cost–benefit calculations) to attract participants in the pursuit of collective goals. Direct participation in the services itself provides the motivation. Participants choose to embody highly cultural, ethical and spiritual values, rather than to accrue worldly goods and material gains. Gülen is against the kind of rationalism that focuses on egoistic self interest and pure materialistic cost–benefit analysis.

166. Is Gülen trying to win a high political or worldly position?

No. Gülen has said, "If I were to prefer this world, to prefer to be at the top of the State, I would have looked for a position in certain places where such preferences could be realized." He has never pursued such goals, but has lived his whole life, including his youth, as an ascetic. Recalling his early years, when worldly prospects were available to him, he says of himself, "If this person refused all the opportunities that came to his doorstep and rather headed for his wooden hut in his youth, how could he have such desires now when he spends every night 'as if this were my last'? I think all of these accusations of seeking position or power arise from the accusers' feelings of hatred."

167. What incentives are offered in the Movement?

For most participants, internalized norms or values are defined by the service ethic, which mostly draws upon religious conviction and conscience and is maintained over time. This means that people work for what are called "value incentives", or "purposive incentives", or "doing the right thing."

The Movement also does not rely on incentives of solidarity, or the self-preservation of the group and its solidarity. If incentives and solidarity were the sole reason for its existence, one could not explain its influence on people in the outside world. There are value incentives and these cannot be explained by self-interest.

168. How are these value incentives used in the relational service-networks and SMOs?

Hizmet enables individuals to expand their cultural co-ordinates and relational networks. For example, people who did not receive an adequate education start giving bursaries to students or start subscribing to magazines and newspapers, or those who have previously had hostile or negative encounters with foreigners or non-Muslims start welcoming them for inter-cultural or interfaith meetings. This opportunity for inner and upward mobility is one of the incentives the Movement provides for all its members. The existence of a network of associations facilitates and supports the development of new leaders for SMOs: socialization within such networks serves as the training ground where skills necessary for the exercise of leadership can be learned. The network cohesion and values encourage the leader-to-be to assume the risks that would be associated with any position. This enhances a strong urge for social mobility among participants in service-networks.

169. Do service-network leaders or participants ever seek or offer particularist rewards?

Inside the Movement the leaders act as circulators of information, different perspectives and experience. In the outside world, they act as representatives of the network(s) and usually project an image of the services with which participants can identify and from which participants draw affective gratification and further incentive.

This leadership and representation provide and require an intensive exchange, interaction and socialization. For many in the Movement the very intensity of exchanges, interaction and participation itself becomes a reward. Therefore, the function of a network leader is to gather and co-ordinate individuals, and to represent projects that the individuals collectively and altruistically work for. This function yields services from which many people benefit and which (according to the orientation of the Movement) God will be pleased with. So the ultimate reward is from God alone and manifold. This is because the participants become the initiator of prolific righteous deeds, as they express their willingness to serve in all parts of the world.

This commitment therefore does not lead participants to seek particularist rewards outside accepted norms and behavior, nor does it lead the network leaders to offer conditional compliance for different demands and isolate some participants.

170. What motivates the individuals in supporting networks to take on roles within the SMOs?

The organizational structure of any SMO maintains its own integration, consensus and motivation. So each SMO tries to provide better, more useful and effective universal services. It does this by making the best possible use of the different resources and talents available to its boards and networks. It pursues shared objectives and adapts to the wider environment. If it provides a series of resources and rewards among its participants, it is done in accord with a formal internal system for the allocation of resources, roles and the division of labor and for the distribution of rewards and sanctions. This sensitivity about resources and their management leads to formalization, openness, transparency, lawfulness and legality. This further motivates the collective actor and individuals in its supporting networks to perform their roles within the limits of both the SMO and the System. Incentives or rewards may range from material advantage, prestige, fraternal bonding, and emotional gratification to spiritual gains.

171. What is the culture, unity and cohesiveness of Hizmet built from?

Availability of information, circulation and diffusion of messages and new initiatives for new service-projects, and the acquired experience and professionalized expertise in the Movement build its culture, its internal unity and cohesiveness. This enables the Movement to maintain the individual and collective need for self-fulfillment, for appropriation and communication of the meaning of action.

ALTRUISM

172. What is the drive behind the institutions and services of Hizmet?

Philanthropy, altruism and voluntarism are the core dynamics of the institutions and services the Movement provides.

173. How does Gülen define philanthropy?

Gülen says philanthropy may assume a number of forms: one's allocation of time, energy, money, or property, or a simple smile, care, or prayers. He sees such provision as an alternative and barrier to egoistic interests at the expense of others, and as a remedy for societal discord, conflict and violence.

174. From where does Gülen derive his views on altruism?

Gülen's approach to altruism is formed by the perspective of Islamic teachings, the Qur'an and the *Sunnah*. The source, origin, consequences and implications of the ideational and social praxis of the Movement are therefore also quite different from those in movements hitherto explored in social movements theory in the West.

175. Is there any difference between the Movement's understanding and other conceptualizations of altruism?

Altruism is an ethical doctrine that holds that individuals have a moral obligation to help, serve, or benefit others, if necessary at the sacrifice of self-interest. There are a great many different perspectives on altruism. Most of the world's religions affirm it as a religious or moral value and advocate altruistic behavior alongside self-discipline and containment of one's own interests and desires. However, psychologists, sociologists, biologists and ethologists have different perspectives on altruism, many of which see altruism as either a form of long-term self-interest or as illusory.

Altruism, from the Islamic perspective, does not hinder individual pursuit of self-development, excellence, and creativity, and it is not an ideological fabrication by the weak for the weak or by the weak to sponge off the strong. It is not like game theory, which discusses the available strategies for each player for a given situation and calculates the average or expected, outcome from each "move" or sequence of "moves." Nor, in the Islamic tradition, is altruism a form of consequentialism, the idea that an action is ethically right if it brings good consequences. What Islam teaches is quite different from what is argued by those who see altruism as a variant of individual or species mechanisms for survival or self-projection.

176. Does Hizmet have a set of working principles?

Yes, the working principles are:

(1) constant positive action that leaves no room for confusion, fighting and anarchy;
(2) absence of worldly, material and other-worldly expectations in return for service;
(3) actions adorned with human virtues that build trust and confidence;
(4) actions that bring people and society together;
(5) sustaining patience and compassion in all situations;
(6) being positive and action-oriented, instead of creating opposition or being reactionary;
(7) collective and consultative decision making;
(8) cooperation/collaboration of like-minded civic people for civilizational projects.

Gülen says that volunteer services offered in this spirit can be said to be seeking only God's approval. He also encourages all individuals in sympathy with his opinions to serve their communities and humanity in accord with this peaceful, non-conflictual, non-confrontational and apolitical stance.

177. How is the relation of education and altruism understood in the Movement?

Gülen has always seen education as being at the center of social, economic and political modernization, progress and welfare. Individuals and society can only be respectful to the supremacy and rule of law, democratic and human rights, and diversity and cultures if they receive sound education. A higher sense of identity, social justice, and sufficient understanding and tolerance to secure respect for the rights of others, all depend on the provision of an adequate and appropriate universal education. So education is the supreme remedy for the ills afflicting society and humanity in general.

As a great many people are unable to afford such an education, they need to be supported by charitable trusts. For these trusts to function well requires the right human resources, that is, dedicated volunteers who enter and then stay in the field of service. The volunteers should not be making a gesture (however worthwhile) but a commitment rooted in sincere intention; their motivation should have no part in it of racial or tribal preferences, and their effort should be both patient and persevering and always lawful. Equity, social justice and peace in one's own society, and in the world in general, can only be achieved by enlightened people with sound morality through altruistic activism.

178. How does Gülen motivate people to offer altruistic services?

One of Gülen's arguments invites people to live and act not for their own present but for the future of later generations. He maintains that people in the present and future generations will pay dearly and not know comfort and contentment if people today do not exert the necessary efforts for the coming generations. Giving examples of characters and events in the past, from Turkish and non-Turkish or from Muslim and non-Muslim history, he has succeeded in awakening a sense of moral duty and obligation, a sense of selfless and generous concern for others. He has used the analogy of a candle consuming itself but illuminating its surroundings.

If people are not financially able to contribute, he asks them to give their time, thoughts, energy and moral support to collective services.

Among the examples he has given are the Biblical Prophets and the Messenger of Islam, their companions and disciples, saintly and scholarly people from global communities, or scientists and community leaders. It is common to encounter names like Newton, Pascal, Sir James Jeans, Kant, Gandhi, Iqbal and Rumi in his writings and teachings.

Gülen also presents the world as a market for humanity's benefit and God's pleasure and says people should compete in righteous and beneficial services without ulterior motives. He urges them to combine their efforts, resources and energies in the field of education into charitable trusts in which no one benefits from the funds the institutions raise except the students themselves. Citing a saying attributed to Ali, the fourth caliph in the formative era of Islam, Gülen holds that "all human beings are one's brothers and sisters. Muslims are one's brothers and sisters in religion, while non-Muslims are one's brothers and sisters in humanity. [...] Human beings are the most honorable of creatures. Those who want to increase their honor should serve this honorable creature."

179. Apart from altruism, do Movement participants have any other reasons for providing services?

Voluntary action in the Movement is justified for the participants by the belief that to act for the benefit of others is right and good and that one has a moral duty to treat others fairly. This moral or philanthropic feature comes from religious inspiration, "serving people, serving God"[1] or "the best amongst you is the one who is the most beneficial to human beings"[2]. Being charitable is a way of life, a way to purify one's intentions, wealth and life.

In addition, Turkish Muslims are undoubtedly inspired by their faith to implement *sadaqa* (charity) and *zakat* (the prescribed annual alms) and set up *vakifs* (endowments, charitable trusts). According to their faith, it is the duty of the affluent to help others and assist the weak, unfortunate, under-privileged, wayfarers, orphans, widows and

---

[1] A universal religious maxim

[2] A hadith

students. The rich person must concern himself or herself with the poor because he or she is responsible for them before God.

Gülen teaches that the path to earn eternal life and the approval of the Giver of Life passes through the inescapable dimension of servanthood to God by means of serving, first of all, one's family, relatives, and neighbors, and then one's country and nation, and finally humanity and creation are the object of one's efforts: "This service is our right; conveying it to others is our responsibility."

As the Movement is now transnational and cooperates with people of many backgrounds and beliefs, participants may have differing motives for their altruism. That is, apart from being a religious duty, altruism is also an act of generosity, an innate feature of being a true human.

Altruism, in general, is a kind of behavior which a) benefits another person, b) must be performed intentionally, c) the benefit must be the goal itself, and d) must be provided without expecting any external reward. With respect to Hizmet, altruistic service outweighs the other dimensions and thus gives the Movement its particular character.

180. What is the value of altruistic services to highly organized contemporary societies?

The presence of altruistic action in the public domain can disclose the existence of hidden dilemmas deeply embedded in the structures and operation of complex societies. Altruism involves putting the interests of others above one's own interests; it demonstrates that people are not inevitably driven by only evident and immediate or even long-term or undefined self-interest. That fact signals the persistence in complex societies of human needs and demands which cannot be reduced to bureaucratic routines and politics.

Altruistic action invites us to seek change and to assume responsibility. It gives individuals a voice in society and a means to bring issues to light; it enables individuals and the public to make a space for difference and to reinforce solidarity for societal peace and cohesion.

181. If the services are philanthropic, altruistic and voluntary, how can they be organized well?

Altruistic action does require some form of organization for its effective performance, but this organization has no need for an institutionalized formal structure and hierarchy. Its ends can be achieved more effectively by informal, diffused, decentralized, permeable networks of friends, business associates or philanthropically like-minded people gathered around a single project, as in the case of Hizmet. That is why so many projects, services, institutions and initiatives of the Movement have come to be supported by such a wide range of individuals, companies and organizations.

182. Does Gülen profit in any way from the services provided?

Gülen owns nothing and has no ambition for worldly wealth. His sincerity, ascetic life style and example of altruism in practice have successfully motivated thousands of teachers as well as parents and sponsors. As a man of profound scholarship and wisdom, a highly gifted writer and speaker, Gülen could well have had a very satisfying career as a community leader and author. However, he has concentrated his efforts on motivating the masses to invest in sound education, and he has led by example. He has always remained aloof from financial management of the institutions and instead encouraged their sponsors actively to oversee the use of their contributions. This has built enormous confidence, not just in Gülen's honesty and integrity but also in that of the people employed at the Gülen-inspired institutions.

Furthermore, the students he has educated and his relatives have followed his example. Aside from never accruing any personal wealth, Gülen is reported to have prayed for his relatives to remain poor so as not to raise any suspicion of their having gained from his influence.

183. Do the workers for the voluntary action not receive any payment in a work relationship?

Absence of direct benefit or direct economic rewards does not mean that the workers for the voluntary action do not receive any payment in a work relationship. However, it does mean that economic interests do not constitute the basis of the work relationship among those involved. Also, economic benefit is neither the cause nor the effect between the voluntary actor and the recipients in the performed action. The voluntary action specifically aims at producing benefits or advantages for subjects other than the volunteers or workers. So its gratuitous nature lies in the free enjoyment or benefit of its product for the recipients. That is why the Movement is generally known as *Hizmet*, a term which means "service to others."

184. Are other benefits forbidden to participants?

No. Beyond the immediate interest of the actor or workers, other "rewards" (symbolic advantages, prestige, self-esteem, authority) are present in altruistic action, just as much as they are in any other form of social exchange. Altruistic action may also yield indirect economic benefits, insofar as the participant acquires useful skills (e.g., professional skills in a certain occupation), establishes networks of influence (professionally advantageous contacts), or learns leadership qualities. Moreover, it is in the nature of such services and of their objectives, that there may be a multiplicity of secondary or tertiary objectives pursued by individuals. Yet these sorts of instances are rather infrequent and do not invalidate the altruistic services undertaken and the collective objectives shared by all those involved to achieve the common good. After all, the inner contentment or repute attached to individuals after such services is not what they aim and work for; these are simply an unlooked-for grace which may (or may not) ensue from doing such altruistic work.

185. How does the Movement nurture professional skills and leadership qualities?

The service-projects and institutions have a corporate identity and their management is in the hands of real people. However, having been appointed as a manager through a contract, these people are not allowed to utilize the institutions for their own benefits. Those who become unable to work actively in the Movement pass their role to newcomers or the next generation who will carry the torch of the altruistic services of the Movement. The activism can be described in terms of a relay race in which the current generation is running and passing the torch on to the next cohort to take it onward and higher. In this way, the consciousness and ethic of responsibility nurtures individual upward mobility.

186. Why are social mobility and professionalization such important features in a social movement based on altruism?

Movement participants have been engaged for a long time in non-formalized, philanthropic or altruistic services. This has led to an extensive cultural training in new (mostly vocational) skills and intellectualization. Hizmet is also strongly committed to professional services, including retraining processes aimed at better-employed actors in the market, projects and institutions.

This social mobility is important for a number of reasons. The most relevant of these reasons for the Movement is that the more mobile a society is, the fairer and more open it is. That mobility has a positive impact on the way networks, projects and institutions are formed, and their size and shape, and the professionalism in them. Well-educated and qualified members doing proficient work incidentally helps promote the image of the Movement within the larger social field.

187. How does altruistic action serve civic and democratizing functions?

Alongside its faith-inspired and humanitarian aspects, the civic aspect is an important feature of altruistic action. This type of action provides far more opportunities for participation than political activities do. Altruistic action expresses membership in a far larger civil community than a political party. It provides people with purpose, a sense of belonging, responsibility, commitment, accountability, with incentives and the inner contentment of trying to be beneficial to others.

Also, since people must reach a consensus on the details of any new social, cultural or educational project, altruistic action performs a distinct civic and democratizing function; people learn how to negotiate and persuade, to present convincing arguments, to be accommodating and flexible about differences, to negotiate, generate and accept consensus. These skills enable to people to live well in democratic societies.

188. Are the education services purely altruistic or does the Movement have other political and material objectives too?

Gülen's understanding of duty, to serve humanity especially in the field of education, permits no expectation of material or political gain. Sincerity and purity of intention should never be harmed or contaminated. Gülen's philosophy of education is not utilitarian, nor a social and political activity which can be divorced from the rest of his philosophy or faith, but a firmly integrated and well-developed component of his worldview. Gülen says that the means must be as valid as the end, and that apparent or material success is not the only measure. The purpose of the Movement is to ensure respect for objective and universal human values, to never have ulterior motives to seek material interests nor to impose any ideology or to seize power through politics in any country.

For over forty years, Gülen has urged his audiences to achieve the right balance of social justice between the individual and community; to develop and advance in every individual and the whole nation feelings of love, respect, altruism, striving for the sake of others and sacrificing their own material and non-material benefits and aspirations for the sake of others. There has never been any evidence of an attempt by the Movement to gain any kind of political power or material objectives in any of the regions where participants work and volunteer.

189. If the Movement is altruistic and peaceful, why does it attract such strong reactions, both positive and negative?

The Movement's understanding of service is geared primarily to altruism in Turkey and abroad. It is a mobilization that presents alternative models of a kind that state systems cannot replicate. That is why it has attracted broad attention, in favor and against, within a short period of time.

The Movement's principle of altruism, of offering "something for nothing" is a symbolic challenge to the dominant cultural codes and the customary (so-called "rational" self-interest) basis of strategic and instrumental logic in complex societies.

The unilateral power of giving (for nothing, sometimes in defiance of immediate self-interest), and in that way generating and providing cultural models, constantly results in a movement's predominance in societies. The reason is that cost–benefit calculations do not motivate or regulate the autonomous and gratuitous ("for nothing") production of cultural models. This means it is hard to side-track or prevent people's ability to produce new and better ways of doing things.

190. Why do some (in Turkey in particular) oppose the Movement?

For those who have exploited and usurped Turkey's wealth and resources for years, the altruism of those raised among the Movement is a challenge to their way of thinking. They have found their logic upset. For they see that while they seek to siphon money and resources illegally from the state and people's pockets, others have begun instead to construct alternate modes of behavior and generate alternative meanings. This offers a symbolic challenge to the more usual rationality of calculation, to established bureaucratic routines, and to means–end relationships. The challenge arises from the given-for-nothing nature of the "offering" and the directness of personal commitment. These two features demonstrate that sharing with others is not reducible to instrumental logic. In essence, the Movement reminds everyone of the limitations of a system's power over people and events. It calls into question the System's sway over us and invites us to assume greater responsibility for our choices and actions. In so doing, it becomes a vital component in the renewal of civil society and the reinforcement of social cohesion. For precisely those reasons there is counter-mobilization by vested interests.

The Movement was able to come through the crisis of the *February 28 Process* without resort to negativity, to any counter-action or conflictual or coercive means. The opposition from certain ideological interest groups within the power establishment in Turkey is directed towards *any* collective actor that is perceived to endanger their schemes and vested interests; however, there are particular reasons why those vested interests made Hizmet a major focus of their counter-mobilizing efforts.

191. Why has such widespread willingness to engage in altruistic action emerged in the form of Hizmet?

Voluntary forms of action emerge as alternative answers to shortcomings, deficiency or crisis in the governmental or welfare system in a society. Whether in man-made crises or natural disasters, people are left to their own devices by mis-direction or absence of welfare provisions and services. People act to provide adequate public goods or services when a system is unable to overcome structural shortcomings by means of governmental institutions. Such conjunctures or opportunities create a feeling that individuals are bound by duty and morality to work towards the common good and common goals. Forms of action then concentrate especially on the issues and fields relating to health, caring, religion and education. All of these conjunctures occurred in Turkey in the twentieth century and Hizmet, which was already in place and capable of taking responsibility, emerged to meet many of society's needs.

192. What characterizes the altruism of the Movement?

The first characteristic is that the action is voluntary and done with no expectation of direct benefit or compensation; second, the single individual freely and voluntarily joins a form of collective solidarity and from personal choice enters a network of relations.

The choice is also marked by unselfish concern for the welfare of others. The altruistic action is characterized by the gratuitousness of the giving – the *pricelessness* of the resources or the time or whatever it is that is given for nothing in return. This gratuitousness binds together the actors involved in it; it evokes solidarity, warmth, affection, mutual esteem, and so forth, amongst all the actors and participants, including both givers and receivers of the services.

THE NATURE OF HIZMET

WHAT SORT OF LEADERSHIP DOES HIZMET HAVE?

193. What does "Hodjaefendi" mean?

It is an honorific meaning "respected teacher." It is an expression of respect for scholarly people and is used for other respected scholars as well as for Gülen. It is not unique or peculiar to Fethullah Gülen. It has no cultic or sectarian connotation or association.

194. Does Fethullah Gülen exercise charismatic authority over the Movement?

No. In the Movement leadership is a group activity. It is based on social influence and revolves around a common task. Gülen himself never assumes, accepts or approves of any of the features which are typical of charismatic leadership styles. There is no claim of charismatic revelation or moments, a sinless start, being born anew, being given rebirth or a new sublime life, or adulation, on or around his name. Neither he nor anyone from the Movement has ever claimed superhuman powers of perception and ability to discern "the truth." The relationship between Fethullah Gülen and the Movement is not based upon intense love for Gülen in person, nor upon his attributes or characteristics, but upon the collective meaning, appeal and essence of the understanding, message, thought and action of the Movement. This does not deny Gülen's immense contribution to the thought and action of the Movement.

195. Does Gülen use the term "Gülen Movement" or "Gülen Community"?

Gülen himself never approves and never uses the terms "Gülen Movement" or "Gülen Community." He prefers the action to be called "the Volunteers' Service" because this does not connote any contentious otherness, political separatism or a conflictual front. He insists that the Movement does not and must not involve conflict, and that the volunteers' service must be offered within a certain framework of principles.

196. Is there central leadership of the Movement?

No. Leadership in the Movement is decentralized. The degree of autonomy of the different components is great, and overlapping of influence can occur. However, while the Movement as a whole is decentralized, its SMOs have managerial organization with positions of authority in their departments.

197. Does Gülen himself express willingness or desire for leadership?

Gülen has repeatedly expressed his reluctance to lead and even his detestation of any leadership or mention of leadership, whether communal, religious or political.

198. What is Gülen's concept of leadership?

Gülen argues that "single-person leadership is no longer viable." He says, "As everything has become so detailed, particularized, specified, and enumerated, tasks now assume such forms that even unique, outstanding individuals cannot accomplish them by themselves. That is why the place of genius has been now replaced by collective consciousness with consultative and collective decision making."

About leadership in Hizmet specifically, Gülen says, "Behind the institutions are many people and companies from almost all walks of life regardless of their worldview, beliefs, and lifestyles . . .What I have done is only encourage people." The assumption that almost a thousand institutions and millions of volunteers and participants in the Movement across the world are governed by Gülen or any other single individual or a specific group of people, is absolutely untenable.

199. How do participants in the Movement view Gülen?

Participants in the Movement tend to appreciate Gülen for his knowledge, scholarliness, sincerity, integrity, commitment to altruistic services, profound concern and compassion for others. It should not be ignored that all these qualities come from his Islamic education and upbringing. However, participants do not perform any sort of sacral celebration of Gülen or any other(s) in the Movement.

200. If Gülen refuses any charismatization and declines any authority over the Movement, what form exactly does his leadership take?

Gülen is best described as a *servant leader*. The qualities that characterize him as a servant leader are:

- self-awareness or awareness of his personal responsibility;
- a primary commitment to serving the needs of others;
- dedication of his life to solving social problems;
- passionate activism;
- being always upright, truthful, trustworthy and just;
- dialogue competencies, communication skills and being an empath listener;
- seeking to convince others rather than coercing compliance;
- effectiveness at building consensus within groups;
- promoting a sincere dialogue among cultures, religions and civilizations;
- profound appreciation of the Islamic sciences and contemporary-modern thought;
- ability to understand lessons from the past without ignoring the realities of the present;
- ability to evaluate the past, present, and future to reach a new synthesis;
- stretching his thinking to encompass broader-based conceptual thinking;
- seeking a delicate balance between conceptual thinking and a day-to-day operational approach;
- being goal-centered and project-oriented;
- doing everything in his power to nurture the spiritual, personal and professional growth of all people within his community;
- building a community based on the principles of servant leadership.

201. Does Gülen intervene directly in service networks or projects?

Rather than direct personal intervention, it is Gülen's intellectual and moral influence that is felt within the Movement. He inspires the Movement; he does not organize it.

202. Has Hizmet produced any self-interested ruling cliques?

Self-interested ruling cliques are typically produced by organizations with rigid forms of authoritarianism and charismatic leadership. Within Hizmet, however, there are no organizational tendencies that prioritize maintaining the organization above every other possible goal. Thus, a contemporary altruistic and cultural movement like Hizmet, which expresses individual or interpersonal relationships and pluralistic and democratic tendencies, cannot produce such groups. So far it has demonstrated no goal displacement.

203. What is "goal displacement"?

Goal displacement is when the elite or leaders come to value leadership and its status and rewards above any commitment to the organization's goals. They tend to look after their private interests and, within the organization, use their knowledge and know-how to influence decision-making processes; subsequently, ordinary members of the organization may be effectively excluded from those processes.

204. What is the purpose of network leadership?

The reason to have network leadership is to negotiate, mediate and facilitate co-operation among individuals and the wider society, not to win membership loyalty or generate propaganda.

Leadership and structures within the Movement are primarily oriented toward carrying out action and service-projects, and so the SMOs have organizational or managerial (not hierarchical) order. There is extensive overlapping of roles and functions in the Movement because participants may belong to several networks or work on more than one project.

Participants' norms include a definition of the relationship between the Movement and society, and in particular a definition of the relationship between the Movement and the participants in its service-networks. The organizational order means that network leaders have to work within these norms.

205. What is the general principle of decision taking in the Movement?

In voluntary services and project-networks a large number of participants gather together in a single or different places and collectively undertake an interchange or consensus on new projects. All alternative actions and considerations are explicitly discussed and any decision is concluded by all participants as a whole. Collective decisions are taken either through consensus or voting.

Organizational forms can therefore be considered to be a strategic choice made by the service-network on the basis of the principles and goals of the Movement. Within the thought and action of the Movement, organizational form and choices are not made by leaders, but by collective social power.

This general principle of decision taking in the Movement is very different from the process in a cadre-type organization. Cadre-type organizations are more fragile and temporary, highly absorbing, smaller in scale and less democratic than a mass membership organization such as Hizmet.

206. How is power and authority sustained or regulated in the Movement?

Supporters' efforts are not coordinated nationally, so autonomy is an important defining feature of service-networks and SMOs generally. This autonomy is achieved through delegation, creation of a specialized body of representatives, and bureaucratic and non-bureaucratic boards based on equality. For a whole range of matters related to the service-projects, decision-making is not concentrated at the top with certain individuals only. There is a continual turnover of network or project leadership. Representatives within networks can be and are called to account at any time. The right to decide belongs to all who come to the network meetings. Free participation and self-motivated input, together with openness and responsiveness to technical and professional expertise, overcome the risk of building up oligarchies and charismatic leaders. All these features sustain and regulate power and authority in the Movement. They require autonomous and conscious decision making and a kind of participation which reflects strong trust in democracy and is a lever for positive transformation.

207. How is leadership practiced in the local service-networks?

As different demands arise, they enter the local decision-making process, which is open to the participation and control of various parts of the network locally or regionally. Continuous, active, democratic, and enduring participation is encouraged, and this does not let a large and inactive base finance a small number of managerial or active leaders, a primary cadre or main organization. The democratic decision-making process naturally prevents any leader or organization from demanding or taking control of an unwarranted or unfair proportion of the resources available within the network. However, this quality of justice or equity within service-projects and networks does not stop people from having various degrees of commitment, specialization, formalization and professionalization.

If we take the educational institutions as an example, they are typically governed by an association which is regulated by law. The members of the association choose a board of directors and a chair person, who all serve for fixed periods. The board meets regularly and must approve all major decisions concerning hiring of teachers, educational curriculum, and policy. Associations in each city or town are responsible for organizing and maintaining their own schools, centers and other SMOs. There is no central record-keeping office for Gülen-inspired institutions and SMOs.

The relationship between Gülen and the institutions and SMOs is one of inspiration rather than direct leadership because the Movement is decentralized. Consensus is as important as inspiration for participants; many participants in centers and schools are there just because they believe in what the centers are doing, not necessarily because they are inspired by Gülen. Some have little or no awareness of Gülen or his teaching.

208. Who can intervene in decision making and control of resources?

The managerial committee or board of any institution or SMO controls the transfer and redistribution of roles, resources and power through processes of collective reasoning. The norms within the service-networks guarantee integration. They provide the critical point of reference for every process of action and transformation. All those who take part in the service-network can intervene in the decision making about control of resources.

In addition to this democratic participation, it is commonly accepted within the Movement that Islam discourages Muslims from actively seeking positions of authority. Campaigning for a position of power may imply that one is enamored of the position for one's own advancement or some other self-serving reason. The Prophetic *hadith* is cited by participants: "Do not ask for a position of authority, for if you are granted this position as a result of your asking for it, you will be left alone (without God's help to discharge the responsibilities involved in it), and if you are granted it without making any request for it, you will be helped (by God in the discharge of your duties)." Thus, within the Movement, authority or power is not seen as something to compete for, and is not often allocated to one who demands or strategizes for it.

209. If the Movement relies on and develops professional expertise, what exactly is Gülen's contribution to its work?

In service-projects, there are people skilled in more mundane tasks of organizing and there are people more skilled in analyzing and expressing needs and intentions. The participants in service-projects organize themselves flexibly. They accommodate and redefine their tasks and inner structures in accordance with feedback from the wider public. They also take into account suggestions from Gülen, if they seek them, and his interpretations of current events through the media, when they are relevant. Participants are clear that there are many sources of opinion and authority available to them. However, this way of working never nullifies or disregards the value and respect attached to Gülen's views and perspectives.

210. Are there likely to be any future conflicts over power, resource distribution or succession in Hizmet?

Since people in the Movement generally avoid seeking positions of power, and participants consciously avoid giving any power to people who seek it, these kinds of conflicts are unlikely to arise. If anyone or any group were to try to raise such conflict, they would be unlikely to win any support in the Movement or have much impact as they would be clearly contradicting the norms within the Movement.

Speculation by outside researchers about potential conflicts over power, resource distribution or succession fails to take account of the activists' own understanding of the opportunities available to them. What such researchers present as the reality has not been mutually and socially constructed and shared between the collective actor and the researcher, so it has no objective reality.

Rather than speculation about future allocation of resources and power, the invisible resources behind the efficacy of the Movement could be usefully studied. These include consensus, lack of competition for power and leadership, various forms of co-operation and exchange, reciprocal interaction, sacrifice, devotion, altruism, and working for and expecting only the pleasure of God. These are the variables by which the Movement achieves its objectives rather than individual or group leadership.

IS HIZMET A POLITICAL OR CULTURAL MOVEMENT?

211. Is Hizmet a political movement, action or actor?

No. A political movement presses for a different distribution of roles, rewards or resources in society and therefore clashes with the power which imposes rules within the structural organization of the state; a non-political movement strives for a more efficient functioning of the system or apparatus of society or, in fact, for that system's more successful outcomes. It does not pass the established limits of the system or its written and unwritten rules, regulations and norms. The Movement fits the description of a non-political movement, so despite being a collective action or mobilization, it cannot be said to be a political movement.

212. What is a mobilization and what kind of a mobilization is Hizmet?

The term *mobilization* is used in general to refer to the action of a group or a group itself which marshals and organizes its resources for use for a particular purpose. This organizing includes the movement of personnel, equipment, supplies, and incidentals to project sites, as well as the establishment of offices, buildings, and other facilities necessary for work on projects.

In this book, when we call Hizmet a mobilization, we are referring to the efforts of the participants to direct resources to achieve their goals in the form of service-projects. Hizmet is a collective social or cultural mobilization.

213. What is the difference between a political and a cultural mobilization?

Mobilizations with political strategies try to change external realities first of all, and they often have defined material objectives; they try to change particular political or economic relations, or particular policy directions or outcomes.

Mobilizations that are culturally oriented, such as Hizmet, tend to look to an interior transformation as a means (and goal) of change in value systems; they aim to preserve or revitalize a culture, and so they focus much more on ideas and beliefs, on values, norms and identities.

214. Why does Hizmet fall into the category of cultural or social actor rather than political actor?

Political actors are classified as interest groups and defined in relation to the government or other politically motivated or oriented entities in a political system, whereas the relevance and interests of social movements extend well beyond those areas to other institutional spheres and authorities. Political actors engage in action for reform, inclusion in and redefinition of the political rules, rights and boundaries of political systems; they therefore interact with political authorities and negotiate or engage in exchanges with them. They strive to influence political decision making through institutional and sometimes partly non-institutional means.

By contrast, non-political actors address issues in a strictly cultural form or cultural terms, and bring issues forward into the public sphere. They choose a common ground on which many people can work together. They name and frame issues in a way that people can understand in the public sphere and then let them be processed through political means and actors.

According to these definitions, Hizmet falls into the category of cultural or social actor rather than political actor. Although political action is legal, legitimate and indispensable for democracy, the Movement avoids formal politics, and acts at its own specific level within the limits to which it is entitled by law, aiming at well-defined, concrete, and unifying goals and services.

215. If it is not concerned with economic and political matters, what does the Movement concern itself with?

Hizmet is concerned with cultural values and beliefs. In its service-projects it incorporates innovations in its established repertoires of action, introduces an element of novelty in its interactions, and establishes a new recombination of identities, methods of serving people, and demands. All these can in turn inspire other movements. Hizmet's concern with cultural and moral values is clearly demonstrated in its intercultural or educational activities and in its transnational altruistic services. It is also clearly seen in its understanding of civil society and pluralist participatory democracy and their compatibilities with Islam.

216. How does Gülen see culture or the cultural dimension of society?

Gülen affirms that the cultural dimension is a necessary component of collective or national consciousness, without which a people cannot move forward along a path recognized and valued as their own. He argues that there is a close relationship between the harmony and stability of the ways in which a people conduct their affairs and their cultural resources. Refusing to see the underlying principles and the components that constitute one's culture is "blindness" and "trying to remove them from society means total confusion."

Turkish society is complex and its needs cannot be expressed without intelligent reference to the cultural resources of its people. The Movement therefore attempts to mobilize the universal cultural elements within the traditions, codes and idioms of the past. On the basis of these it develops ways of thinking, speaking and acting that can stand out as independent and free of control and standardization by the traditions, codes and idioms that at present are imposed on people in Turkey and elsewhere.

217. Does Hizmet's cultural understanding make it exclusivist?

The fact that most societies are complex and not homogenous – they contain people of different classes, ethnic groups, religious backgrounds, etc – means that it is possible to find elements and values that cultures and the people within them have in common. Because it actively seeks these common grounds, Hizmet has participants from across all segments of Turkish society and has quickly become transnational. It now has supporters and participants from a great many ethnic groups, nations and of varied religious and philosophical views.

Within Hizmet all of these people are able to inquire into and express their views on the relation between faith and reason, and on peaceful coexistence in liberal democracies with religious diversity, education and spirituality. It is clear then that Hizmet is not in any way exclusivist.

218. Hizmet has clear effects on Turkish society, so how can it be said to be non-political?

A notable feature of the Movement is that participants acknowledge and abide by the political system, and display disinterest towards seizing power and gaining control over the state apparatus. Hizmet assumes forms of action and organization which are accountable and amenable to political mediation by the Turkish political system, without becoming identifiable with it. The Movement therefore does not act like an oppositional action which involves a minority, or which rejects the system in Turkey, or which resists the "rationality" of decisions and goals imposed by the Turkish system. The Movement is a cultural actor, or a social movement, *not* a political movement.

The chief implication of the Movement is that political parties are unable to give adequate expression to collective demands. This is because parties are structured to represent interests that are assumed to remain relatively stable, with a distinct geographical, occupational, social, or ideological base. Also, a party must ensure the continuity of the interests it represents. When faced with the task of representing a plurality of interests, the traditional structure of a party may not be able to adjust itself to accommodate them. Indeed, a political party can hardly mediate between short- and long-term goals. For short-term gains and profits a party may act in favor of unstable, partial and hierarchical interests. In contrast, unlike political parties and bodies, Hizmet's participation in social projects and in the specific areas of social life demonstrates no interest in hierarchism or short-term gains.

219. Does Hizmet favor any political party or "wing" of politics?

There is no political wing, party or umbrella organization of the Movement. It does not have cliques or a radical-flank effect[3]. It has not become divided into radical and moderate factions. There has never been an extreme, radical or political group that defines the parameters of the Movement.

Hizmet represents its understanding through formal institutions. As these institutions are mostly educational, they do not take sides with political parties. Thus, the Movement cannot be said to be based on, influenced by, affiliated with, or supporting the interests or policies of any single political party.

---

3 The 'radical flank effect' is when political bodies set up or support moderate competitors to more radical groups. The political bodies do this to reduce support for the radicals and prevent reduction in the numbers and effectiveness of their own supporters.

220. Has Hizmet ever formed an alliance with a political party?

No, the Movement has never allied itself with any established political party. This independence has secured it a certain measure of success. Although Hizmet originated as a faith-inspired initiative, participants see that their faith does not need control of a state or political party to survive, but does need the educated, the financially well-off and a fully democratic system.

Gülen's ideas differ clearly both from those of ultra- and neo-nationalists, and from political and moderate Islamists in his emphasis on the entrance of Turkey into mainstream global processes and a market economy and his stress on intellectual development and tolerance.

221. Do Gülen and the Movement harbor aspirations to evolve into a political party or gain political power?

Gülen and the Movement do not have any such aspirations, as has been observed and repeatedly confirmed by Gülen and participants, and by many observing scholars and journalists. On the contrary, Gülen represents the continuation of a long Sufi tradition of seeking to address the spiritual needs of the people, to educate the masses, and to provide some stability in times of turmoil. Like many previous such figures, he is wrongly accused of seeking political power.

222. If it is not through gaining control of the System or government, how does Hizmet influence society?

The established social practice of the Movement focuses on the role and needs of the individual. It emphasizes individual needs for self-reflexivity and self-realization. Without straying into forms of narcissistic behavior, or the individualistic search for self-affirmation and instant gratification, Hizmet testifies to a profound change in the status of the individual and his or her problems. Through socio-cultural efforts and services, the Movement addresses the individual dimension of social life, and thus with the products it provides, it may then affect the whole of society. Its space and the level where new forms of social action originate is not political space or power, nor government, nor regime. It educates and socializes individuals without individualizing and politicizing the social.

It acknowledges that neither individuals nor a system ever undergo change at all levels at the same time and in the same way. Change requires a lengthy period of time, enormous sacrifice, commitment and patience, and it can be achieved only through education, peace and the co-operation of like-minded citizens and civilizations.

In a contemporary reformulation of the teachings of Rumi, Yunus Emre, and other classical Sufi teachers, Gülen emphasizes the self-development of heart and mind through education. He encourages engaging proactively and positively with the modern world. He advises reaching out in dialogue and a spirit of cooperation between different religious communities, social strata and nations.

Gülen has concentrated his efforts on establishing dialogue among the various ideologies, cultures, religions and ethnic groups of Turkey and of the wider world, far beyond traditional religious circles alone.

223. What social fields do the SMOs work in?

They focus on education, health, media, publication, ethical finance and humanitarian aid and relief.

224. What is the approach of Hizmet to cultural activism?

Gülen does not ask individuals to remain passive recipients, just accepting whatever is fed to them from the outside. Rather, he advises them actively to seek possibilities and alternatives to construct themselves. Both means and ends must be non-confrontational, non-violent and non-coercive; they must be grounded in love of human beings and the creation. They must be based on reliable information and understanding through education and communication. They must founded on freedom, collaboration and peace.

Hizmet's *modus operandi* is to fashion new meanings for social action and to serve as a vital engine of innovation. The Movement sees that the needs of the individual, culture and society, come before politics. However, this should not be in any way confused with naïve culturalism that may ignore rights and guarantees recognized by political institutions. Hizmet's action then contributes to a redefinition and reshaping of what democracy is, can be, and ought to be.

225. How does Hizmet differentiate between cultural and political action?

The Movement's discourse and practice demonstrate a consistent understanding of the separation between the cultural efforts and actors that can bring an issue to light and the political efforts and actors that may then carry that issue into the political arena. The Movement's worldview and habitual or customary social practice demonstrate that it is not a political actor and that it systematically differentiates between socio-cultural issues and political action.

Through the outcomes of institutionalized social projects, Hizmet turns into a catalyst allowing societal needs to be seen and analyzed within new conceptual frameworks. Those outcomes prove that the level of individual meanings and cultural dimensions is more significant than the political level. Such dimensions and meanings are often not easily and quickly identifiable, so politics and politicians can ignore and eliminate them from their analysis between election periods.

The Movement highlights the importance of an open civil society and public spaces because these provide an arena for the consolidation of democratic institutions and for the peaceful encounter between politics and social movements and altruistic services.

226. Does Hizmet engage in political rhetoric or partisan politics?

The character of the services (that the participants are engaged in providing) keeps them away from the everyday and largely pointless partisan fights and rhetoric of political parties; participants do not divert or exhaust their energies in political skirmishes. The effectiveness of Hizmet's activities arises from its openness and receptiveness, and the efficiency of available forms of representation. This quality of Hizmet contradicts the dominant understanding of social movements in the West, which sees movements as always contentious and conflictual.

The Movement's conscious avoidance of political contention reflects Gülen's evaluation of the failures in the last few centuries in Turkish history. He has been critical of those past failures and indicated what he believes to be the reasons for them: "Those who were in politics and those who supported them considered every means and action as legitimate and permissible if it would gain position for their own team or party; they devised and entered into complex intrigues and deluded themselves that by overthrowing the dominant group and changing the party in power they would change everything and the country would be saved. Action should have been guided by thought, knowledge, faith, morality and virtue rather than by political ambitions and hatred." Thus, rather than any kind of politics, it is the religious and cultural vision of Hizmet that is central to its activities.

227. Is Gülen concealing his true intentions or hiding political intent?

No. Gülen has been accused of politically motivated subterfuge, of concealing his true intentions, of hiding a political intent and agenda. For instance, in 2000 a state security court prosecutor accused Gülen of inciting his readers to plot the overthrow of Turkey's secular government. However, Gülen described the charges as fabrications by a "marginal but influential group that wields considerable power in political circles," and in 2006 he was acquitted on all counts.

Gülen says he is "not seeking to establish an Islamic regime but does support efforts to ensure that the government treats ethnic and ideological differences as a cultural mosaic, not a reason for discrimination. Standards of democracy and justice must be elevated to the level of our contemporaries in the West."

228. How does Hizmet respect differences between people?

The Movement's established practice and appeal prevent it from identifying itself with or as a specific political individual or actor. By acknowledging everyone as they are, and by giving everyone the chance to be different and respected, the collective actor of Hizmet cancels out its own separateness. Through its inclusive and integrative action, the Movement proposes being for others while being itself. By contrast, a political actor proves its separateness, restrictedness or exclusivity and guarantees itself first. The political actor first guarantees being for itself, mostly in a contentious way, while being different, visible and separate from others.

IS HIZMET A SECT OR CULT?

229. Is membership of Hizmet exclusive?

No, the Movement does not have membership as such, let alone a closed membership. The Movement encourages participants to be open to the world, to be active in and belong to many, diverse networks, and benefit from social and intellectual mobility; it urges continual access to sources of information, ideas and arguments outside itself, and co-operation with others on the basis of universal values.

230. Is the Movement a Sufi tariqa?

A *tariqa* is a Sufi order. A tariqa has a shaykh, a *murshid* or "guide" who plays the role of leader or spiritual director of the organization. A tariqa consists of a group of *murid*s, (*murid*, Arabic for 'desirous of knowing God and loving God'). In most cases, during his lifetime the shaykh nominates his successor who will take over the order. Every tariqa has a chain or lineage of shaykhs. Every murid on entering the tariqa is assigned daily recitations authorized by his murshid (usually to be recited before or after the pre-dawn prayer, after the afternoon prayer and after the evening prayer). Usually, these recitations are extensive and consist of reciting a certain formula at certain times. The recitations change as a student (murid) progresses from being a mere initiate to higher levels (usually requiring additional initiations).

Being in the spiritual tradition of Islam loosely referred to as Sufism, tariqas provide accepted avenues for expressions of faith. Tariqas have spread to all corners of the Muslim world. It is important to note that membership of a particular Sufi order has never been exclusive and cannot be likened to ideological commitment to a political party. Unlike Christian monastic orders which are demarcated by firm lines of authority and sacrament, Sufis are often members of more than one order. The non-exclusiveness of Sufi orders has important consequences for the social extension of Sufism. Tariqas are a cumulative body of tradition, rather than individual and isolated experiences, and mostly refrain from indulging in direct politics. They are seen as preventing Islam from becoming a cold and formal-istic doctrine by constantly infusing it with local and emotionally popular input, including deductive stories, fables and rituals, which literalists see as not part of Islam proper.

Hizmet, on the other hand, is not a Sufi tariqa. Gülen does not function as the shaykh (Sufi master). Unlike in classical tariqas, there is no requirement of initiation, no restricted or esoteric religious practices, procedures, ceremonies and no arcane mystic terminology that marks membership in the Movement. The Movement does not fit into any characterization of a tariqa in any classical social or organizational sense.

231. Does the Movement have any private, exclusive, sacred texts, rituals and priestly functions, or special costumes?

The Movement does not have or seek to have private sacred texts exclusive to itself; it does not have or seek to develop special rituals and priestly functions, or special costumes or gestures or insignia, or other devices that help to form a closed identity for a group. It does not offer outcomes or rewards unattainable by the ordinary means of human effort in the real world. It does not seek sacral celebration of the self in an abstract and anachronistic paradigm. The Movement's action is not directed *against* anyone, real or mythical: it has no fantasized "adversary" to blame if there is any shortfall in outcomes. Rather, any failure must be socially defined within the actors' frame of reference and responsibility.

Instead of blaming other people or groups for social problems or individual failings, Gülen identifies phenomena and personal qualities to be combated. He attributes all the trouble in modern Turkey to three things: ignorance, poverty, and internal schism (social disunity). He has commented, "Now to these have been added cheating, bullying and coercion, extravagance, decadence, obscenity, insensitivity, indifference, and intellectual contamination....A lack of interest in religious and historical dynamics, lack of learning, knowledge, and systematic thinking [...] ignorance, stand as the foremost reason today why Turkey and the region is so afflicted with destitution and poverty."

232. Why are Movement participants sometimes perceived as stealthy or cautious in interaction with others?

Movement participants are aware that outsider-researchers' interpretations of their discourse and action may, when reported, harm an institution or voluntary body in which they work. This is because of the sensitivities of the Turkish state and political system (in which the balance of power can shift abruptly and unpredictably) and the current world situation related to Muslims or Islam-inspired movements. This leads people to a prudent caution in expressing ideas which, if recorded in any way or published in a biased and malicious manner, may later bring unwanted consequences or distortion or dismissal of their own understanding of what they are doing.

233. Why do some Turkish critics of the Movement describe it as a sect?

Turkey is a secular state in which freedom of conscience and association are conceived in such a way that religious communities and religious orders (because not regulated by the state) at the time of writing do not officially exist. At the beginning of the Turkish Republic a number of new restrictions were placed on religious orders or tariqas, faith communities (including Muslim, Christian and Jewish), and on the practice of religion by ordinary members of the public. Nevertheless, faith communities and religious orders not only survived but they have revived and gained prominence in Turkey. Modern institutionalization and organization in Turkey in fact remains backward, while religious brotherhood and solidarity, basic forms of social organization, continue. Indeed, those basic forms of organization, bottom–up, civic, faith-inspired initiatives, constitute the necessary social capital and resource for modernization in the country. Their success is nevertheless viewed by the protectionist elite with suspicion and described as a potential or actual threat to the foundations of the state.

The Turkish Constitution's commitment to *laicism* means that people can be (and many people have been) prosecuted for affiliation to and support of religious orders or sects. As there is no ethical charter accepted by all actors in the Turkish political domain, the ensuing moral emptiness means that much of the political domain has become "the space of dirty tricks and duplicity [and]...the source of corruption."[4] Politics in Turkey is, regrettably often, based on what are euphemistically called "protective relationships", for the sake of which the concepts of both religion and secular democracy are misused. Thus, in Turkey the terms "sect" and "cult" are used indiscriminately by *laicist* critics to disparage faith-groups or communities.

In this socio-political context, the accusation that Hizmet, while non-political, is a sect, backward, and thus subversive is one of the devices used to delegitimize it and the services its participants provide. Yet, while accusations of this kind have been plentiful, evidence under Turkish law of unlawful association, action or conspiracy by the Movement is non-existent. Ideologically motivated prosecutors and the protectionist groups behind them have laid charges against Gülen and Movement participants, but they have never achieved a conviction against a single person from the Movement.

In repeated investigations, the authorities have concluded that there is no sign in Gülen's works of supporting the interests of a religious sect, seeking the establishment of a religious community, or using religion for political or personal purposes, or of any violation of basic government principles and order. Gülen's works consist of explanations of the Qur'an and Hadith, religious and moral advice, and writings that encourage the virtues of good, orderly citizens.

234. Are there any grounds on which the Movement can be described as a sect?

No, the Movement does not fit any of the criteria which are used to identify sects or cults. The Movement has never attempted to form a distinct unit within Islam. It is not a distinct unit within the broader Muslim community by virtue of certain refinements or distinctions of belief or practice. It is not a small faction or dissenting clique aggregated around a common interest, peculiar beliefs or unattainable dreams or utopia.

---

4 M. H. Yavuz, & Esposito, J. L. eds. *Turkish Islam and the Secular State: The Gülen Movement.* Syracuse, Syracuse University Press, 2003, xxii.

The Movement is already a well-established and transnationally recognized diffused network of people. It has no formal leadership, no shaykhs and no hierarchy. Participants do not undergo any procedures, ceremonies or have to pass any initiation in order to be affiliated or to take part in activities.

In wider Turkish society, Movement participants are not viewed as and do not act as any kind of closed, special group. Movement participants, with their words, projects and actions, have proved that they do not have any strongly held views or ideology that are regarded as extreme by the majority in Turkey and abroad. The public, the media and the courts do not regard them as heretical or as deviant in any way. Movement participants have not been accused of practicing anything different from the generally accepted religious tradition.

235. What stops the Movement from becoming a cult or sect?

One common characteristic of participants in the Movement is their acceptance of the scholarly authority of Gülen. They tend, in addition, to emphasize particular aspects in the practice of their faith. These aspects emerge as distinguishing features or styles in their positive discourse and peaceful action. However, certain factors disable any sort of retreat into a closed group or sect. These include the Movement's consciousness of moral and religious values, and its ethics of responsibility towards Turkish and global human societies, the spirit of competitiveness and upward mobility, and the encouragement to acquire knowledge from multiple sources outside the Movement.

The Movement does not attempt to distinguish and then cut itself off from the Muslim or secular global communities by a distinctive ideology, myth or utopian vision. The Movement has no special doctrines or dogmas, no private texts or procedures, no rites, ritual, insignia, costumes or ceremonies that mark people as having "joined." Indeed, there is no membership, properly speaking, and certainly not an exclusive one.

Leadership is decentralized, resource management and decision-making are diffused through institutions. Institutions are in regular, informal touch with each other, but they are formally and operationally independent. The institutions and activities of the Movement are open to all. The institutions and activities provide scientific education, sound moral teaching based on universal ethical values, and they encourage peaceful, positive activism, and civic engagement for everyone's community and humanity.

The Movement is not linked to any sectarian tradition or affiliation. Networking, participation and affiliation in the Movement are not exclusive, alienating and sectarian because the Movement is not closed to the outside world; indeed, it intends collective engagement with the wider public. This is evident in its extensive, intercultural and interfaith activities and organizations throughout the world. It has no closed orientation either of a geographical, communal or ideological kind, but has an open and fluid structure.

236. Do participants see Fethullah Gülen as a kind of "charismatic" leader?

Charismatization is a process that occurs inside sects and cults. It is a process that makes the group leader a special being, even a super-being in the eyes of cult members; it includes constructing myths about a leader's childhood, sacralized places, holy objects he has used and touched, etc. A picture is built up of a super-being who is prepared to come down to the level of ordinary people. Charismatization by his followers makes the group leader unaccountable, unpredictable, arbitrary in the exercise of authority and prone to abuse of power. Having this power and being unbounded by rules or tradition, the leader can dictate or interfere in what his followers do in all aspects of their life – whom they will marry, whether they will have children or not, what sort of work they will do, where they will live, perhaps even whether they will live – right down to most trivial details of their lives. This authority applies to everything and the leader can change his decisions and commands at whim and at a moment's notice.

In stark contrast to this kind of charismatization, Movement participants clearly do not accord this type of unbounded and arbitrary authority to Fethullah Gülen. Though everyone who knows and comes into contact with Gülen recognizes and respects his knowledge, asceticism, piety, expertise and scholarliness on religious, spiritual and intellectual matters, this does not result in any sacral recognition or charisma for Gülen. The common description of Gülen as the leader of the Movement – something that he himself has never accepted or approved – has not resulted in the emergence of an authoritarian personality or personalities. The Movement has remained committed to the establishment of collective reasoning, consultation and consensus, which prevents the emergence of or lapse into herd mentality or "group-think."

237. What does Gülen mean when he speaks of a "renaissance"?

Gülen frequently talks about a renaissance, but by this he does not mean any sort of magical "rebirth." On the contrary, this renaissance is an active process and involves toiling to "prevent illnesses like passion, laziness, seeking fame, selfishness, worldliness, narrow-mindedness, the use of brute force" and to replace them "with exalted human values like contentedness, courage, modesty, altruism, knowledge and virtue, and the ability to think universally."

The Movement is attached to rationality through its acknowledgement of differences and multiplicity in society, the necessity of division of labor, and its recognition of power relationships within the larger community. Its rationality is geared toward assessing the relationship between ends and means, and toward protecting people from the imbalances and divisions created by the forms of power required to manage complexity. Far from teaching people to expect some kind of sudden, magical transformation, in his written and spoken words Gülen constantly exhorts participants to greater effort, greater knowledge, and greater self-control and restraint.

238. Does Gülen propose a return to Ottoman patterns?

No, Gülen does not propose a nostalgic return to Ottoman patterns. His references to history contain no hint of cultural politics. He makes no attempt to disparage any historical epoch, especially not those moments associated with the origins of modernity in Turkey. He does not evoke the past in order to express a wish to restore the sultanate as a shortcut to unity and order, nor does he idealize "homeland", "religion", and "family" for a cause. He recognizes and understands the complexities of the modern world.

Since the inception of the Movement, Gülen has presented models for self-improvement leading to social transformation. He does not see the past as a strategy for reinforcement of the present political order, nor does he consider that a new model based upon the past can or should be reinstated in the present. In fact, he has called that kind of thinking a grotesque anachronism, and said that no sane person could believe that such a jump in time could come to fruition. In his view, Turkey will not regain the transnational hegemony it exercised before the First World War. To Gülen, the very idea of such cultural imperialism is incompatible with current economic, military and geographical realities. The Movement and Gülen's efforts are very different from reactionary projects which seek to revive or restore the past. Gülen repeatedly affirms that "if there is no adaptation to new conditions, the result will be extinction."

Gülen looks to the past for examples to follow and mistakes to avoid; that is, he looks to the past for the means to go beyond what has remained in the past. He has said, "Today, it is obviously impossible to live with out-of-date conceptions which have nothing to do with reality. Continuing the old state being impossible means either following the new state or annihilation. We will either reshape our world as required by science, or we shall be thrown into a pit together with the world we live in."

However, being aware of history clarifies the concepts of the present that are mostly shaped by the concepts and the events of the past. On this topic, Gülen has said, "If keeping your eyes closed to the future is blindness, then disinterest in the past is misfortune." By presenting a very broad range of historical themes and characters, Gülen instills hope and gives his audience access to the necessary measures for reform and advancement in globalized society. To him, knowing history is the road to an innovative and successful future in which people are able to know where they are going.

239. What is Gülen's attitude to commemorating or celebrating events and people of the past?

Gülen emphatically refuses the model of citizenship that reflects a certain kind of racial, ethnic, cultural and religious homogeneity based on some (often imaginary) society in the past. In point of fact, he stresses that none of the seventeen states that the Turks historically established were based on any such homogeneity. Gülen has argued that consoling oneself with re-telling the heroic deeds of others indicates a psychological weakness peculiar to the impotent who have failed or who are refusing to shoulder their present responsibilities to the present society. He says, "Of course we should certainly commemorate the saints of our past with deep emotion and celebrate the victories of our heroic ancestors with enthusiasm. But we should not think this is all we are obliged to do, just consoling ourselves with tombs and epitaphs. ... Each scene from the past is valuable and sacred only so long as it stimulates and enthuses us, and provides us with knowledge and experience for doing something today. Otherwise it is a complete deception, since no success or victory from the past can come to help us in our current struggle. Today, our duty is to offer humanity a new message composed of vivid scenes from the past together with understanding of the needs of the present."

240. Is the Movement's understanding of cultural values and history a kind of regressive utopianism?

The Movement does not follow any anachronistic paradigm in the way that cults do. It does not romanticize the past. Yet it does emphasize cultural values. Gülen has said, "Little attention and importance is given to the teaching of cultural values, although it is most necessary to education. If one day we are able to ensure that it is given importance, then we shall have reached a major objective."

This emphasis on cultural values has been seized upon by critics who describe it as a reactionary call to return to pre-Republican Ottoman society – in sociological terms, a kind of regressive utopianism. The term of abuse employed in the Turkish context – *irticacı* – can be translated as "reactionary." However, Gülen has always denied this accusation: "The word *irtica* means returning to the past or carrying the past to the present. I am a person who has taken eternity as a goal, not only tomorrow. I am thinking about our country's future and trying to do what I can about it. I have never had anything to do with taking my country backwards in any of my writings, spoken words or activities. But no one can label belief in God, worship, moral values and . . . matters unlimited by time as *irtica*."

Hizmet has never defined its identity in terms of the past, not at its inception and not at later stages. It does not draw upon or create an escapist myth of rebirth. Its action does not rest on a utopian appeal with religious or ideological connotations. It does not reduce the complexity of modern life to the unity of a single all-embracing formula. It acknowledges different levels and tools of analysis, and therefore does not identify the whole of society with the sacral solidarity of any group. Its religious accent does not make it susceptible to manipulation by any power structure, to marginalization as sects, or to transformation into a fashion or commodity for sale in the marketplace as a mind-soother. Competition in and among the service-projects does not allow the Movement to be led or to change into an individual flight, a mythical quest or fanatic fundamentalism.

241. Is the Movement closed off from the world?

The Movement is not closed off from the world because it knows that it needs to be in the world in order to learn from it. Instead, Gülen urges inclusivity and openness to other people. He explains, "People must learn how to benefit from other people's knowledge and views, for these can be beneficial to their own system, thought, and world. Especially, they should seek always to benefit from the experiences of the experienced." Individuals who have been reading and listening to Gülen are therefore unlikely to enter a sect-like relationship or structure.

242. Do Movement participants draw back into the group and break off relations with others?

The cohesiveness of the group, in contradistinction to cults, does not derive from belonging to it. Belonging is not for its own sake; that is, it is not turned inward, but for the service of others, and always looking outward. Motivation and incentivization are realized through the relational networks and the services provided altruistically alongside others. This is what ties individuals together.

Gülen often refers to a Turkish maxim: "An individual should be among the common folks like any ordinary individual, yet with the constant consciousness that he or she is with God and under His constant supervision." This means living among people and amidst multiplicity or diversity. Therefore, unlike sects or cults, Movement participants prefer being with and for people, not avoiding them; they do not draw back into themselves and break off relations with social partners, or sever relations with the outside, nor do they renounce relevant and feasible courses of action.

Gülen stresses the interdependence of communities that have emerged with modern means of communication and transportation, and that the world has become a global village. He teaches that any radical change in one country will not be determined by that country alone because this epoch is one of interactive relations, so nations and peoples are more in need of and dependent on each other. This situation requires closeness in mutual relations, and people should accept one another as they are and seek ways to get along with each other. Differences based on beliefs, races, customs and traditions are richness, and should be appreciated for the common good through peaceful and respectful relationships.

Gülen points out that "this network of relations, which exists on the basis of mutual interest, provides some benefits for the weaker side. Moreover, owing to advances in digital electronic technology, the acquisition and exchange of information is gradually growing. As a result, the individual comes to the fore, making it inevitable that democratic governments which respect personal rights will replace oppressive regimes."

243. Is the worldview or collective action of the Movement an isolationist withdrawal into a pure community-based structure?

A sect creates ideological and existential separations, divisions and ruptures that cannot be overcome. Its identity politics and appeal tend to cover up or deny the fundamental dilemma of living a social life in complex systems. Being an exclusivist organization, a sect demands a long novitiate, rigid discipline, a high level of unquestioning commitment, and intrusion into every aspect of its members' lives. If a society or people that are searching for fulfillment within specific closed networks find themselves unable to handle the flow of information that they are exposed to, they withdraw from social life and transform their spiritual needs into intolerant mysticism. If a movement's identity claims are pushed too far, the movement eventually evolves into a conflictual sectarian organization with an intolerant ideology; the movement then tends to fragment into self-assertive and closed sects. If certain issues or differences become political and contradictory, and if the movement's political decision making is limited and incapable of resolving the differences, it breaks up into sectarian groupings.

The worldview or collective action of the Gülen Movement, however, is completely different from that of a sect. It is not an isolationist withdrawal into a pure community-based or sect-like structure. Gülen recognizes and welcomes the nature of social life in today's complex global systems. He has said, "We should know how to be ourselves and then remain ourselves. That does not mean isolation from others. It means preservation of our essential identity among others, following our way among other ways. While self-identity is necessary, we should also find the ways to a universal integration. Isolation from the world will eventually result in annihilation."

Hizmet participants find fulfillment within service networks and are enabled to handle information flow more comfortably. They therefore do not withdraw from social life, and their spiritual needs are not transformed into intolerant mysticism. Since participants' identity needs and claims are not pushed too far by an intolerant ideology in service networks, the Movement does not evolve or fragment into a conflictual, self-assertive and closed sect or any kind of sectarian organization. Since issues or differences in the Movement are not politicized but are handled with a cooperative rather than conflictual attitude, and since decision making is collective and consensual, the Movement remains capable of resolving the differences arising from multiplicity in complex societies. This is why Hizmet has never broken up into sectarian groupings.

244. Is Gülen developing a separate or special group?

About being or becoming a sect, Gülen has said that he is "personally not in favor of such practice." He says that Movement participants "do not represent a separate and divisive group in society," and they "are not associated with any group, nor have developed such a group."

The Movement is different from a sect or separate group in that it operates in awareness of its commitment to the social field where it belongs, interacts and contributes. It shares with the rest of society a set of general issues, and seeks to find and form common grounds and references with others. Gülen writes, "Huge developments in transportation and telecommunication technology have made the world into a great village. In these circumstances, all the peoples of the world must learn to share this village among them and live together in peace and mutual assistance. We believe that peoples, no matter of what faith, culture, civilization, race, color and country, have more to compel them to come together than what separates them. If we encourage those elements which oblige them to live together in peace and awaken them to the lethal dangers of warring and conflicts, the world may be better than it is today."

245. Does Hizmet activate negative or destructive processes?

The Movement does not have an ideology which posits an "adversary" as an object of aggression, and which denies that adversary any humanity or rationality or potential for good. The Movement systematically and consistently refuses to activate negative or destructive processes. It has for that reason sometimes been criticized for passivism. However, that is not a valid criticism either. In fact, the Movement encourages a higher motivational level and opens the way for individual and collective responsibility and mobilization. Gülen teaches that the principal way to realize projects is "through the consciousness and the ethic of responsibility. As irresponsibility in action is disorder and chaos, we are left with no alternative but to discipline our actions with responsibility. Indeed, all our attempts should be measured by responsibility."

246. Does Hizmet produce unpredictable forms or expressions of collective action?

Because it correctly and accurately identifies the true social character of conflicts, the Movement avoids producing unpredictable forms or expressions of collective action. Movement participants are socially, culturally, and intellectually competent, so they can respond to the specificity of individual and collective demands. In this way they do not allow demands to cancel one another out. They do not try to escape into a reductionism that ignores or annuls the individual for the appropriated identity of the Movement. Utilizing this social capacity, the Movement does not lapse into less social or less cooperative types of behavior, or withdraw into a sect or dissolve into a utopian myth.

247. Has Gülen led anyone into deviations of any sort?

Gülen has been visible in public life through his speeches, actions, and projects since he was sixteen years old as preacher, writer and the initiator of civil society action. He has not led anyone into any absurdities, deviations, violence, killings, suicide or abuse of any sort. He has not presented any attitude of unaccountability or arbitrariness in his thoughts or actions. In Turkey a few marginal, ideologically motivated individuals and groups have opposed his worldview and projects, yet none so far has substantiated any accusation like this. This is a good indication that Gülen and the Movement do not resemble the sects, cults or new religious movements studied by contemporary scholars.

248. Does Hizmet deny diversity and interdependence?

No. The Movement does not deny the interdependence of the social field in its worldview, values, or actual organizational frame. It does not have a totalizing ideology that possesses and controls the social field; and so it does not need to identify "others" or "outsiders" in negative terms.

Sects, by contrast, resist accepting difference and diversity within themselves and resist accepting their interdependence with the outside world. They lack a solution for handling difference within complexity.

Their totalizing appeal does not take into account that people are simultaneously living in a system interdependently.

249. What saves the Movement from turning into an authoritarian, totalizing organization?

People in the Movement take part in society in many ways and within many different relationships. These inclusive and multiple affiliations link and integrate different areas of the Movement. This therefore allows different individuals in service-networks to come into personal contact with one another. While establishing bridges between SMOs, individuals share and exchange experiences, resources and information. Private, cultural and social dimensions intersect in multiple but compatible (usually complementary) participations in the Movement. Such freedom of choice and action, with inclusiveness and flexibility, blurs boundaries between the Movement and wider society, and contributes to the growth of channels of communication, interaction and mutual trust. This is what saves the Movement from turning into a single, authoritarian, all-powerful, totalizing, sectarian organization and prevents the development of such leadership.

250. How does the Movement deal with new information and change in general?

With its participation in the fields of education, interfaith and intercultural issues, and transnational altruistic projects and institutions, the Movement proves itself able to process information and emergent realities. It acknowledges the fact that the common points, grounds, references and problems affecting humanity in general are far more than the differences which separate us. Gülen teaches that "one can be for others while being oneself", and "for peaceful coexistence, one can build oneself among others, in togetherness with others." The difference and particularism of an actor do not negate interdependence and unity with others. People can come together and co-operate around a universally acknowledged set of values. The way to do so is through education, convincing argument, peaceful interaction and negotiation.

IS HIZMET CONFLICTUAL OR VIOLENT?

251. Is Gülen a revolutionary?

Gülen is non-political. He does not want to politicize Islamic values and is seen as a reformist thinker rather than a revolutionary. He seeks to address the spiritual needs of the people, to educate the masses, and to provide some stability in times of turmoil. It is wrong to accuse him of seeking political power.

252. What is Gülen's attitude to conflictual action?

A conflict is a struggle between two actors seeking to appropriate or control resources that are regarded as valuable by both. Gülen takes no part in such conflicts. He argues that "for a better world, the most effective path must be to avoid argument and conflict, and always to act positively and constructively," and, "in the modern world, the only way to get others to accept your ideas is by persuasion"; "those who resort to force [are] intellectually bankrupt; for people will always demand freedom of choice in the way they run their affairs and in their expression of spiritual and religious values." While it still needs to be improved, "democracy is now the only viable political system, and people should strive to modernize and consolidate democratic institutions in order to build a society where individual rights and freedoms are respected and protected, where equal opportunity for all is more than a dream." Gülen asserts that conflictual or reactionary action cannot reach its goals precisely because it typically offers extremism and violence and begets counter-extremism and counter-violence.

253. Is the Movement conflictual? Does it breach any limits or laws?

The actors in a conflict have a shared field of action, a common reference system, something at stake between them that both groups refer to implicitly or explicitly. The adversaries enter into strife because of antagonistic definitions of the objectives, relations, and means of social production at issue between them. The conflict manifests as a clash over control and allocation of resources that are deemed crucial by the concerned parties.

However, Hizmet is not an expression of a conflict. Participants do not break the limits of the system of social relationships in which their service project or efforts are located. They do not infringe the rules of the game, and they are always willing to negotiate about the objectives of institutions or service projects that they have set up or are running. The Movement does not contest the legitimacy of power or of the system in which it has emerged. Its collective action is not class-based, politically oriented, contentious or adversarial. It does not have narrow material objectives.

The service of the Movement has never combined with or been infiltrated by marginal and deviant groups present in the societies where the institutions set up by participants are located. The educational services have never dissolved into mere claimant behavior or violent rupture, nor lost the capacity to tackle educational issues for the common good.

Hizmet works to resolve ignorance, backwardness, disunity, unbelief, injustice and deviations. So it does not concern itself with offering any political challenge to the legitimacy of power or to the current deployment of social resources. So the Movement cannot be defined as a conflictual or confrontational reaction.

However, Gülen and the Movement do address and try to deal with problems or crises – problems such as the attempted politicization of religion, societal and sectarian tensions and exploitation thereof to keep Turkey off balance. Hizmet also opposes undesirable activities such as fundamentalism, dogmatism and coercion, but participants do not try to control specific individuals or groups or political parties or the state.

254. Is Hizmet a claimant movement?

No. A claimant movement seeks to defend the advantages enjoyed by a separate group or to get a bigger piece of the "cake" of public funds or other resources for an underprivileged ethnic, religious, social or political group. Hizmet does not do this, so it cannot be described as "claimant."

The Movement does not mobilize for political participation in decision making, nor does it fight against the state ideology, nor does it pretend to have a bias or tendency in order to get access to decision makers. Movement participants have contributed to the opening-up of new channels for the expression of previously excluded demands like intercultural and interfaith dialogue and co-operation (rather than conflict) between civilizations. However, they do not in any way push their service outside the limits set by the existing norms and political system. They also do not seek to change the regime or the democratic parliamentary system or otherwise intervene in its decisions or actions. Not every public-spirited action is political or antagonistic; rather, there are social, cultural, cognitive, symbolic and spiritual dimensions of such action that can never entirely be translated into the language of politics.

255. Isn't the Movement antagonistic in character?

No. The collective action of the Movement may put pressure on the political market, but this pressure is not necessarily demand-oriented or antagonistic. In the Movement, there appears the dimension of *offering*, a kind of action which develops and anticipates new models of social rationality. This action concerns cultural codes, not confrontation and conflict with the political system. It allows ordinary people to take back responsibility for a variety of different roles in service to society. Indeed, the very identity of the Movement depends on its success in providing services for communities.

The principles and goals of Hizmet do not permit any sort of aggressive or non-institutionalized mobilization. The Movement does not permit impractical and incompatible demands or expectations, or anything transgressing boundary rules – either in the Turkish or the international arenas – that could trigger conflict. Movement participants are encouraged to reflect upon and compare their action in different situations at different times; there is an open process of working out costs and benefits, of measuring effort and outcomes, that enables them to criticize and amend policy, to predict likely outcomes, to learn from mistakes, etc. In this way, the institutions, the services given and their success, do not belong to any single individual. Instead they remain oriented outward to the real world.

256. So why do some critics see the Movement as antagonistic?

The social centrality of the Movement, the autonomous role in defining personal needs, the constant mediatory relationship between welfare, health, education and the individual, family, and community, gives everyday experience a function. This situates action along the continuum ranging from difference to innovation or change, to the creation of new arenas for positive action and culture. Dominant groups and interests may have neglected or may still be neglecting these arenas and so may see such change and innovation as threatening to their political control or their interests and therefore as explicitly antagonistic in character.

257. Has the Movement ever turned to direct action?

No, it has never turned to direct action, nor threatened to turn to it. In all domains, the Movement has consistently rejected the use of civil disobedience, confrontational or direct action tactics. It has instead focused its energies on establishing new enterprises and co-operatives, agencies for personal development, in-service training, and job placement. It has proved able to unite and mobilize large numbers of people from many diverse backgrounds to work on significant social projects. This is evident in sectors such as education, journalism, television production, radio broadcasting, co-operatives, the accommodation industry (building houses, hostels and hotels), health therapy, aid and relief organizations, and banking/finance. Accordingly, one of the effects of the Movement has been modernization of society through the expansion of innovative occupational sectors, with notably high turnover of personnel in communications, education and welfare services.

258. Is the Movement reactionary?

In conflictual actions or networks, action is taken by simpler and small "cells" against the rules that govern social reproduction in everyday life. These cells go on to generate networks of conflictual social relations and a variety of forms of resistance. Naturally there are forms of such popular and ideological resistance in Turkey, but this activity or behavior is absent in Hizmet so the Movement cannot be accurately deemed reactionary.

Gülen asserts that conflictual or reactionary actions – or movements, no matter how powerful they are – cannot be successful in achieving their purposes because balance and moderation cannot be maintained in them. Quite the opposite, conflictual and reactionary actions prove to be very harmful as people fall into extremism. This extremism then causes strong reactions on the other side. Violence ensures counter-violence from the others, too. What is essential, what ought to be, is positive action.

259. Is Hizmet an extreme right-wing attempt to defend the social order?

Hizmet does not breach the system limits in order to defend the social order, as in the case of ultra right-wing counter-movements or fascist movements. The Movement does not claim, compete for, or raise conflict over something within the state organizational or political system.

Since it is not a struggle or mobilization for the production, appropriation, and allocation of a society's basic resources, and since it is not engaged in conflict over imbalances of power and the means and orientation of social production, Hizmet is not materialistic or antagonistic. It does not dispute the shared rules and the processes of representation. It does not dispute how normative decisions are made through democratic institutions.

Hizmet aims for the internal equilibrium of society. It aims for exchange among different parts of the system, and for roles to be reciprocally assured and respected so that social life, fairness and the material and non-material prosperity of individuals are maintained and reproduced through interaction, communication, collaboration and education. These relations allow individuals to make sense of themselves, of this world and its affairs, and of what lies beyond it.

The Movement takes no direct interest in institutional change or the modification of power relationships. Rather, it aims to bring change in the individual, in mind-sets, attitudes and behavior. The many forms of the voluntary and altruistic community action undertaken by Movement participants correspond to everyday life and are strictly cultural in orientation, not political.

260. Is Hizmet trying to change the rules of the political system?

The activities of the Movement take place within the confines and rules of the political system as it is. They do not aim to maximize the advantages of the actor in political decisions. No matter how their worldview or services might empirically affect the political system, they do not threaten to disregard or infringe the rules of that system as given, nor do they transgress its institutional boundaries.

The services given by the Movement are not a contest among adversaries for control over the allocation of social production. They are not a struggle of imbalances of power among social positions. Rather, all the efforts of the Movement need to be analyzed using analytical categories other than political ones, for example, as collective social altruism.

Rather than advancing political ambitions, Gülen's objective is to foster an ethic that some social researchers have characterized as coming very close to Max Weber's "worldly asceticism," an activist pietism with a tendency toward the rationalization of social relationships. Researchers also attribute the protectionist groups' suspicion about the Movement to the protectionist's underlying power interests.

261. Are Gülen and Hizmet secretly working toward the foundation of an Islamic state?

No. The discourse and actions of the Movement – their teaching and projects within Turkish social and cultural life – do not transgress any procedural or institutional boundaries. Their services and organizations do not break the rules of the political game or the acclaimed secularism in Turkey. On the contrary, Gülen has even been feted by Turkey's secular establishment. The message he preaches is one of tolerance, promoting a non-politicized form of Islam which can peacefully coexist with Turkey's strongly secular state.

262. Did the February 28 Process provoke the Movement into a situation of crisis or conflict?

The February 28 Process severely challenged and tested the unity and identity of Hizmet as a collective actor and the firmness of its hold on its worldview. However, the Movement was able to respond positively and peacefully, and preserve its coherence in each of the spheres in which it provides services. This most serious situation failed to initiate a breakdown or fragmentation of Hizmet or any breach of its external boundaries.

263. Is Hizmet subversive?

No. What is common to all projects, services and institutions of the Movement is that they are entirely located within the limits of compatibility of the System. They are not oriented towards conflict or breach of those limits. Gülen-inspired institutions are never brought into conflict with the state. None of the projects in which Hizmet participants are involved ever break the rules of society, nor do they try to change "the rules of the game" no matter what field they are concerned with.

Hizmet does not do anything which prevents the system from maintaining its set of elements and relations that identify the system as such. Since participants and their projects do not breach social limits, the system can acknowledge, or tolerate, them without altering its structure. In this sense, Hizmet has order-maintaining orientations. However, it does not come into being through consensus over the rules governing the control of valued resources. The intention of the Movement is not to protect the status quo governing the control of valued resources; nor does it emerge to challenge the rules and procedures which protect that status quo.

Hizmet is not marginal as it did not come into being to react to the control and legitimacy of the system or its established norms; it is not a consequence of the inadequate assimilation by some individuals of those established norms. Moreover, Hizmet does not identify a social adversary and a set of contested resources or values. Within the Movement people express disapproval of actions or traits such as immorality, unbelief, injustice, provoking hostility and violence, and deviations, but disapproval or hatred is not expressed of the people who engage in them.

264. Is Hizmet's innovative potential subversive?

No. The Movement's innovative potential is not subversive. Based on Islamic teachings, Gülen encourages people to offer services which are not an opposition to interests within a certain moral framework. Services offered do not seek to improve the relative position of the Movement actor so that the actor will be able to overcome functional obstacles in order to change authority relationships.

265. When Movement participants define their kind of altruistic behavior as "competition for the good or better," what do they mean?

The behavior they are describing in this phrase concerns not contending interests but presenting the likely best that can be done for the betterment of the conditions of society and humanity. Such competition accepts the set "rules of the game" and is regulated by the rights people are entitled to and by the interests that operate within the boundaries of the existing social order. Such competition is indeed different from those forms of solidarity action which force the conflict to the point of infringing the rules of the game or the system's "compatibility limits."

This is supported by the results of surveys conducted by independent organizations, by the ever increasing recognition and acceptance of the Movement's cultural services and educational institutions in Turkey and abroad, and by the failure of the legal actions taken by the protectionist elite in Turkey against Gülen.

266. Does participation in service-networks encourage or enable individuals to challenge the law?

Integration or participation does not in any way prompt participants in Hizmet to breach the limits of the System. While seeking integration to the Movement individuals are not required, or allowed, to challenge the constraints established by law or the general public. The history of Hizmet so far has not shown any illegality.

It is through micro-relational mechanisms (that is, friendships, acquaintance, associational networks, and kinships) that people are motivated to join the Movement. These mechanisms reduce the cost of participation and encourage people to mobilize themselves without law-breaking or risky behavior.

267. Does Hizmet break off relations with social partners in the wider public?

The Hizmet Movement as collective actor does not draw back into itself or break off relations with social partners in the wider public. The strategy or relationship of Hizmet is therefore integration with and full commitment to the wider society through educational and cultural institutions and community work, rather than isolation, alienation and withdrawal from it.

268. Does the lack of conflictual activity in Hizmet cause it to be passive?

Communication and interaction is free-flowing among individuals, networks and SMOs within the Movement. Collective judgment, sensitivity and legality are used to the full so as not to embarrass or upset participants and sympathizers of the Movement and others who are neutral to it. This is believed to be vital, especially for transnational educational services. This cooperative attitude should not be mistaken for passivity or lack of assertiveness.

In fact, through forbearance and patience, participants are able to transform conflictual potential into productive resources for and through the services they deliver. The Movement shows that mental, material, moral and spiritual transformative energies can be channeled into development without deviating into conflicts and violence. (That, incidentally, is evidence of capacity to learn from the experiences of political engagement of other collective actors, past and present).

269. What are participants' attitudes towards diversity and coexistence?

Gülen has explained, "The peace of this (global) village lies in respecting all these differences, in considering these differences to be part of our nature, and in ensuring that people appreciate these differences. Otherwise, it is unavoidable that the world will devour itself in a web of conflicts, disputes, fights, and the bloodiest of wars, thus preparing the way for its own end."

In all circumstances around the world, Gülen and Movement participants act meaningfully to reduce aggression, adhering to a simple maxim of paramount value: "Peace is better." Gülen and the Movement prove definitively that they are on the side of peace at home and abroad offering Muslims a way to live out Islamic values amidst the complex demands of modern societies. They offer Muslims a successful way/model to engage in ongoing dialogue and co-operation with people of other religions.

270. How does Hizmet respond to provocation coming from outside agents?

Hizmet is quite unlike exclusive, ideological solidaristic organizations with limited material and ideational resources. In the latter, organization is based upon symbolic incentives – either ideological or solidaristic: such incentives prove a significant surrogate for lack of material resources. Such organizations are at any time liable to use violent and coercive means. This becomes ever more likely as the rigidity of their organizational model or structure increases.

For some forty years now, the collective action of Hizmet has shown no such tendency, nor been tempted in that direction. If any individual in the Movement has felt tempted to violence in response to provocation coming from outside agents, the Movement has successfully contained such impulses. The verbal and written discourse of the Movement has been and is available to all and shows no sign of condoning or inciting even disruption, still less violence.

271. What prevents Hizmet from turning into a fundamentalist or regressive sectarian organization and from breaking up into conflictual factions?

The Movement stays well clear of ritual or sacral affirmation of any ideological principles or leading personalities. This prevents the radicalization of the image of the action beyond its factual meaning and contents. The project-networks or SMOs of the Movement are not contentious subgroups. They are not unresponsive to important needs in the wider social or political arena, inside or outside Turkey. Besides, there are no networks or SMOs that have broken away from the Movement after deviating, nor are there any opportunist leaders. There is no likelihood of such an eventuality. All these characteristics prevent Hizmet from turning into a fundamentalist or regressive sectarian organization and from breaking up into conflictual factions.

Instead, individuals in Hizmet mobilize themselves into an action or movement that is non-conflictual and peaceful. Through the Movement, individuals attend constructively to the branches and roots of the crises afflicting their society and humanity.

IS HIZMET ANACHRONISTIC?

272. Aren't faith-based movements such as Hizmet marginalized, alienated, and anachronistic these days?

The Hizmet Movement is faith-inspired but not faith-delimited. It cannot be said to be marginalized, alienated or anachronistic because it is actively engaged in Turkey and world-wide. It successfully engages in establishing collaborative relationships through dialogue and joint projects with like-minded individuals and institutions of different religious and cultural backgrounds. It is in this sense a thoroughly forward-looking movement concerned to contribute constructively to the mainstream.

273. Doesn't a faith-based or faith-inspired movement such as Hizmet lead people to fundamentalism?

Quite the contrary. What Gülen started and the action of Hizmet can lead to a much sounder deterrence against religious fundamentalism than anything which the state has produced as a deterrent. The door Gülen opened can give ordinary people the opportunity to live Islam peacefully within their own individual and collective identity. To enable people to do this, at the same time as securing peace and tolerance amidst diversity and pluralism in complex societies, faith or religion needs to be protected by contemporary peaceful thinkers and useful institutions. Gülen-initiated dialogue and reconciliation meetings and their positive outcomes have taught many people about this need and convinced them to cooperate for the greater good.

274. Did Hizmet emerge to oppose the modern world?

No. Hizmet is a service movement that arose from civil efforts and projects in which Islamic morality and ethics responded constructively to development and global challenges. The Movement promotes morality and service ethics that aim to fuse with, rather than combat, the socio-political needs, developments or institutions of the contemporary world. In an order open to civil society, initiatives like Hizmet should lead to reform and improvement of local and national decision-making processes, and standards of democracy and social justice.

275. Does Hizmet aim to express and reinforce old-fashioned and conservative patterns in society?

No. Although the values expressed by Gülen and Hizmet are traditional, the work of the Movement, as demonstrated by its sustained outcomes, leads steadily and reliably to modernizing innovation, to more balanced distribution of opportunity and effective welfare services. The scale and professional quality of the services managed by Movement participants, outside as well as inside Turkey, have been widely acknowledged. Their administrative and operational successes have been achieved in extremely competitive environments, and sustained for over thirty years.

The successful secular education provided by the Gülen-inspired secondary- and tertiary-level institutions, the service-ethic mind-set associated with universal moral values grounded in Islam, combined with the cultural and professional training gained in both the receiving and the providing of modern education, has led to a marked horizontal and vertical social mobility in Turkey. It has contributed, in short, to a modernization of society – that is not something that could have been anticipated by the protectionist and vested interest groups within the power establishment in Turkey; it is an outcome that runs counter to their assumptions (and prejudices) about any mobilization that strives to make an intelligent, enriching use of the human and cultural resources of the lands and history of the Turkish people.

However, the positive outcomes of Hizmet's work can hold only so long as the state does not impose a bureaucratic centralist approach on society as a whole. Such an approach extends arbitrary controls (for example, raids into civil society SMOs by legally unauthorized military personnel), impedes participatory processes and the democratic rights expressed through those processes, but strengthens the protectionist mechanisms and exclusivist values that make society less and less "open."

276. How does Gülen reconcile tradition and modernity in his teachings?

Modernity has forced individuals and groups into an anxious state of rapid change and uncertainty. It has radically drained and emptied the individual's life of the symbolic functions which used to enable social expression, imagination, and aspirations for successful integration into the social fabric. Gülen's work focuses on precisely this integration or reintegration, taking on the task of healing the breach and remaking one's world. It teaches both the theoretical and practical aspects of how to become a rounded human being, how to educate the mind, heart and spirit in order to lead a fulfilled life and be oneself while being with and for others. Gülen makes the modern condition meaningful by a mixture of conservative thought and liberal tolerance that encourages people to adopt new ways of *naming* or defining and perceiving reality. His thought favors individual modesty, social conservatism and Islam in the founding of civilization, and he gives examples of modest and tolerant people who have not lost their connection with God, as well as examples of individuals who have been worn down by modern excess and the suppression of tradition.

277. How does Hizmet act to counter the negative effects of modernity?

Turkey is a country where the nation state has so far not been able to fully integrate its citizens or to meet the demands of society at large; for various reasons – poverty, education, ethnic or religious difference

– large sections of the population still experience alienation in relation to the institutions of the nation-state. This is often compensated for through ethnic, local and/or family ties.

Besides such ties of family and ethnicity there are other relational networks through which Hizmet acts to counter alienation, such as weekly neighborhood meetings, professional associations, parent-school associations, charities and so on. The Movement's operational values such as consultation and collective decision making, collective ownership, and community also counter the alienation which modernity brings. In interpreting and tackling the problems of modernity, the Movement helps to formulate solutions at the level of individual autonomy that can prepare for the development and integration of the individual into the modern nation-state and life in the twenty-first century.

278. How exactly does Hizmet integrate the individual into the modern nation-state?

Compared to mobilization and struggle based on reactionary, political and antagonistic interests, Hizmet has distinguished itself as an enduring form of service network. It interweaves closely with the daily life needs and identity of the wider community it serves. This has transformed a potential that was latent into visible collective action. The civil society networks of the Movement prove themselves mediators and enablers, rather than blockers or retarders, of the civilizing process. They help to find solutions to the problems of modernity at the level of individual autonomy. This allows the development and integration of the individual into the modern nation-state and helps wider society to adapt to the complex industrialized society that occurs in modernity.

279. How does the Movement help wider society to adapt to modernity?

The Movement presents to the wider society new cultural, organizational, and relational models. It teaches individuals to use their constitutionally given rights to contribute to and serve society positively. In general terms, Hizmet is best described as "a form of collective, purposive, and organized social altruism that has arisen from civic society." Non-profit services are sources of diversity and innovation which provide both people and policymakers with the vehicles, alternatives, models and solutions to deal with social ills.

280. What is Hizmet's relation to globalization?

Part of Hizmet's reputation is owed to the success of the collective services by institutions and SMOs outside Turkey. Its transnational and joint projects have yielded significant recognition and co-operation from foreign sources. That success in part motivates the counter-mobilization against the Movement in Turkey.

The business, educational and interfaith organizations operating across economic, political and cultural boundaries work within a common rationale based on knowledge, skills and shared ethical values. The core of the Movement is an educative mobilization which addresses time, space, relations between people, the self, and the affective deep structure of individual behavior. Its rationale therefore does not exhibit change, whether in Turkey or anywhere else.

Hizmet's service projects and networks successfully open possibilities for new solutions by getting people together to talk about vital issues in their communities. In this way the Movement helps to produce insights and solutions for common issues and common concerns. It therefore works to connect to actors who are responsible for those key issues, or more correctly for solutions. This also leads to mutual understanding of differences and ways to act positively, constructively and peacefully even with those differences; it prepares the ground for complementary action and mutually respected collaboration for the greater good in a globalized world.

WHAT IS HIZMET'S RELATION TO DEMOCRACY?

281. Is Gülen an Islamist?

Gülen refutes in his speeches and writings Islamist claims for an Islamic political platform: "Islam does not propose a certain unchangeable form of government or attempt to shape it. Instead, Islam established fundamental principles that orient a government's general character, leaving it to the people to choose the type and form of government according to time and circumstances."

Gülen's rejection of Islamism is not due to merely strategic considerations or even personal preference. Rather, it is based on the argument that the Islamist claims to have found political guidance in Scripture represent a gross misunderstanding of the nature of the Qur'an that dangerously distorts the believer's approach to it. Gülen says, "Such a book should not be reduced to the level of political discourse, nor should it be considered a book about political theories or forms of state. To consider the Qur'an as an instrument of political discourse is a great disrespect to the Holy Book and is an obstacle that prevents people from benefiting from this deep source of divine grace."[5]

Moreover, Gülen rejects the totalizing ideological character of Islamist political thought and activism as totally foreign to the spirit of Islam. Islam advocates the rule of law and explicitly condemns oppression against any segment of society. Gülen holds that democracy and Islam are fully compatible and that Islam prescribes no particular form of governance, certainly not arbitrary rule, and that the central Qur'anic message is that Muslims must take responsibility for their own society. He teaches that Islam promotes activism for the betterment of society in accordance with the view of the majority. This activism complements democracy rather than opposing it: "This understanding of Islam may play an important role in the Muslim world through enriching local forms of democracy and extending it in a way that helps humans develop an understanding of the relationship between the spiritual and material worlds. I believe that Islam also would enrich democracy in answering the deep needs of humans, such as spiritual satisfaction, which cannot be fulfilled except through the remembrance of the Eternal One."[6]

In addition, Gülen is critical of the instrumentalization of religion in politics, and has no direct participation in party politics

---

5 An Interview with Gülen by Zeki Toprak & Ali Ünal. *The Muslim World Special Issue*, 95(3), 447–67, 2005: 456.

6 Ibid., 452.

because the modern world exists in a pluralistic experience rather than within an assumed homogeneity of truth. He is against those who have created a negative image of Islam by reducing Islam to an ideology. Through words and deeds he underlines the distinction between Islam, a religion, and Islamism, a profoundly radical political ideology that seeks to replace existing states and political structures, either through revolutionary or evolutionary means. He opposes the use of Islam as a political ideology and a party philosophy, and the polarizing of society into believers and nonbelievers. He calls for those who believe and think differently to respect and tolerate each other, and supports peace and reconciliation.

282. Is Gülen practicing taqiyya (subterfuge) in his rejection of Islamism?

No. Gülen is not merely pretending to reject Islamist ideology. He has clarified publicly in print and broadcast media that he and Turkish Muslims, like all Sunnis, do not have this concept of subterfuge or dissembling in their faith and practice, nor do they condone it .

Any accusation of subterfuge is symptomatic of the grossest oversimplification of the socio-cultural and spiritual dynamics of the Movement; it contradicts the consciousness and clear understanding of the growing number of supporters of the Movement (now in their millions), which is very strict in its critique of conditions in the countries where Islamist groups condone subterfuge as a tactic.

There are good reasons for being confident that Gülen is not a secret Islamist and that he rejects Islamist epistemology. For instance, before and after 9/11, Gülen visibly provided intellectual and moral leadership, condemned all kinds of acts of terrorism with the most courageous and unequivocal public statements, and comprehensively explained related and relevant issues. He stated that the basic principles of religion are totally opposed to the political–ideological interpretations that underlie and motivate acts of terrorism; that these basic principles should be taught to Muslims and other people through the education system; that administrators, intellectuals, scholars and community leaders have a responsibility to try to identify the originators and the motivating factors behind terrorist activities; that there are multinational organizations which, overtly and covertly, have directed their efforts to destructiveness and the creation of fear in society.

283. What is Gülen's view on mixing politics and religion?

Politicizing religion is always a reductionist endeavor: it turns the mysterious relationship between humanity and the Divine into an ideology. Gülen says, "Religion is the relationship between people and their Creator. The feeling of religion lives in the heart's depths. . . . If you turn it into a display of forms, you'll kill it. Politicizing religion will harm religion before it harms a government's life." He has also said, "Religion focuses primarily on the immutable aspects of life and existence, whereas political, social, and economic systems or ideologies concern only certain variable social aspects of our worldly life."

Being careful not to politicize religion does not mean religious people should be indifferent to what goes on in the public sphere, or to political or economic injustice. Gülen is not arguing that religious or spiritual people should stay out of the political arena or stop concerning themselves with politics. Such a recommendation would be no better than quietism and is a withdrawal from the responsibilities and obligations of citizenship and social participation. Political involvement and advocacy is not the same as partisanship and party loyalty. Religion can and should speak publicly regarding political issues that affect human dignity and welfare, environmental stewardship, social justice and peace. Truly religious people who are responsibly involved in their polis are not single-issue voters or single-party loyalists. They are not involved in dividing but in building communities and societies.

Gülen holds religion to be far above politics; he sees it as a source of morality and ethics, which are relevant to, not in conflict with, responsible politics. He does not want religion to become a tool of politics because when politics fails and goes awry, people may blame religion. He does not want political aspirations to blemish religion or their potential for corruption to degrade it.

284. What is Gülen's understanding of democracy?

Gülen directly criticizes Islamist political thought in his many books and articles and argues in favor of democracy and the modernization and consolidation of democratic institutions in order to build a society where individual rights are respected and protected. He carefully makes clear his position that some forms of democracy are preferable to others and is cautiously optimistic about its development: "Democracy has developed over time. Just as it has gone through many different stages, it will continue to evolve and improve in the future. Along the way, it will be shaped into a more humane and just system, one based on righteousness and reality. If human beings are considered as a whole, without disregarding the spiritual dimension of their existence and their spiritual needs, and without forgetting that human life is not limited to this mortal life and that all people have a great craving for eternity, democracy could reach the peak of perfection and bring even more happiness to humanity. Islamic principles of equality, tolerance, and justice can help it do just this."

285. Is Gülen in favor of the principles of liberal democracy?

Gülen has always been in favor of democratic institutions, free elections and other principles at the core of liberal democracy today. He maintains that the Qur'an addresses the whole community and assigns to it almost all the duties entrusted to modern democratic systems; he says that people ought to co-operate by sharing these duties and establishing the essential foundations necessary to discharge them, and that government is composed of all of these basic elements. He says, "Islam recommends a government based on a social contract. People elect the administrators and establish a council to debate common issues. Also, the society as a whole participates in auditing the administration."

286. What is Gülen's attitude to the democratic initiatives in Turkey since 2000?

Rather than leave Turkey to remain a closed society, Gülen has long supported initiatives for a democratic, pluralistic and free society. He states that the role of individual morality is pivotal in this perspective to build, strengthen, and preserve a just political order. In the same vein, he has supported ties to the West – on the basis that Turkish society has much to gain from the achievements of rational knowledge there – whereas many from both the religious circles and the dominant secularist elite have been opposed to such rapprochement. Gülen was among the first and strongest supporters of full European Union membership and integration, although some Islamist political groups criticized his remarks and opposed such membership. To them, the European Union is a Christian club and a threat to Turkish national and Muslim identity.

Gülen was gradually able to bring about changes in the public mentality and attitude in Turkey. He supports democracy and tolerance as the best way to govern and supports membership in the European Union as the best way of achieving economic prosperity. In addition, he has highlighted the need for peace, tolerance, and dialogue with ethno-religious minorities within the Turkish community and between nations as an integral part of Islam and Turkish Muslimness.

287. Why does Gülen support the state, even when it has been oppressive?

Gülen asks people to be careful to respect the values and authority which the state or state organizations ideally stand for. He has spoken out against those who cause chaos, societal tension and violence in Turkey or anywhere else. He argues that while dealing with tarnished politicians, crooked party politics and corruption, people ought to pay extra attention not to erode in public respect for a state organization.

Gülen is aware of the risks brought by a failed or failing state to a population, nation and region. For this reason, he warns that anarchic movements and activities destroy the atmosphere of peace, free exchange of ideas, and the rule and supremacy of law and justice: "I have always stipulated that 'even the worst State is better than no State.' Whenever I voiced my opinion in words such as 'the State is necessary, and should not be worn down' I have never sanctified the State as some people have done. This preference is a necessity for me because if the State were not to occupy a certain place, it is certain that anarchy, chaos and disorder would dominate there. Then, there would be no respect for ideas, freedom of religion and our consciences would be violated; justice would be out of the question. In the past there were times when our nation suffered from the absence of the State. Therefore, I regard supporting the State also as a duty of citizenship."

288. How does Gülen affect the consciousness of people about the state and democracy?

Gülen calls for democratization, freedom, equity, justice, and human rights and the rule of law as the main basis for the regulation of the state–society relationship. This call has symbolically confronted the privileged role and vested interests of the protectionist elite in Turkey. He has brought about a shift toward civil society and culture, rather than party politics, as new reference points in the mind-set and attitudes of Turkish people. Therefore, although he is not a politician, he is influencing people's consciousness in ways that will affect the future of Turkish democracy.

289. How does Gülen prioritize the democratization, industrialization and economic development of Turkey?

Gülen argues that through the democratization of Turkey it is possible to keep together industrialization, economic development and a form of nondependent participation in the world system. He believes democracy and development are interdependent and equally important, but democracy precedes development.

He works for the development of a society freed from hunger, poverty, striking inequalities and suppression of civil rights. This can be reached only if, along with economic development, society guarantees improved forms of civic as well as political participation, equal rights, and respect for civil and cultural freedom. He does not want change to lead to decreased participation and deeper isolation in the current world system. Without democracy, Turkey cannot conceive development in any meaningful sense. To Gülen, efforts to bring about transformation in institutions and the established mind-set in Turkey should be made through education, interaction, collaboration and consensus, without resort to violent or coercive means and ends.

290. How does Gülen believe civil initiatives can bring about positive change?

Gülen encourages non-confrontational, non-conflictual efforts to serve one's community, nation or the whole world. He asks people to persevere without modification in these positive efforts, despite peculiarly difficult conditions or adverse situations. He holds that this will allow Turkey to participate in the world system, not in a merely dependent position but with some capacity to exert influence and engage in dialogue and negotiation. By the same token, he sees this as a condition also for making a contribution to democracy on the world scale.

To Gülen, the democratization process may thereby draw attention to critical weaknesses and inadequacies in political initiatives aimed at the problems and issues facing us today. It is therefore one of the roles of social movements to bring these issues to public attention, through the proliferation of information and its novel forms and alternative projects and altruistic services. Gülen believes that cultural activities and non-violent forms of action, provided they find the proper channels, can sometimes reach out to address the world and make the difference. He maintains that today such positive change can only be brought about partially and in a piecemeal fashion.

291. What is the stance of Hizmet on Islam and secularism?

Modern Turkey is unique in the Islamic world in its aggressive, totalizing approach to secularism and secularization. Like many in Turkey, Hizmet is deeply critical of the positivistic character, undemocratic impositions and non-egalitarian application and practices of Turkish militant secularism. But it is a major misreading to conclude that it is opposed to secularity and democracy. In fact, Hizmet is precisely the sort of movement that offers Turkey's best hope of reconciling Islam, modernization, and secular, liberal democracy.

The collective mobilization of the Movement continues to this day because the actor has succeeded in realizing – and through the course of action continues to realize – a measured integration or harmonization between many contrasting requirements. As long as secularism is understood and practiced in the best way, or at least as it is in the most industrialized democracies of the world, the majority of the Turkish population, including Hizmet participants and supporters, will continue to support it.

292. How does the Movement encourage and enable coexistence?

One problem humanity faces at the global level has to do with the way in which we can coexist and develop common goals while respecting indelible differences. In order to act collectively at any given time, it is necessary to define a concept of "we"; however, this definition is not likely to be set once and for all, but has to be agreed upon over and over again in a continual negotiation.

The Movement's ongoing projects, the ever-increasing number of educational institutions, the cultural and dialogue centers, and the non-profit, non-governmental organizations, are all important civic initiatives constituting this continual negotiation.

293. What place can a faith-inspired movement like Hizmet have in a pluralist democracy?

The Movement contributes to the achievement of the conditions necessary for an effective pluralist democracy through formal and informal networks such as conferences, platforms, relational and associational neighborhood meetings and media outlets. The majority of the Turkish media support the Movement's initiatives, regardless of their origin and almost all state and political leaders and intellectuals have expressed their approval and appreciation. All these indicate the Movement's contribution to a pluralist society and democracy.

294. Is Hizmet's contribution to society and democracy recognized by all social actors in Turkey?

Its contribution is recognized by most, but not all social actors in Turkey.

A particular emphasis of the approach and actions of the Movement is being in the service of the common good, not in the service of a private cause. Hizmet affirms its belonging to the shared culture of the society and its acceptance of the political and cultural diversity of Turkey. It does not deny others' identities. It refuses adversarial discourse and contentious action, whether lawful or unlawful. In return, it is widely acknowledged as living fruitfully in and contributing to secular and religiously plural democracies.

Nevertheless, the protectionist elite in Turkey does not recognize the Movement except as "the adversary." This hostile reaction reduces the potential for positive, fruitful interactions; it indicates a failure of political (as well as moral) imagination, and a readiness to conceive difference only in terms of conflict. The harm in this attitude lies in the tendency of conflict – whether it concerns material or symbolic resources – to transgress the system's shared "rules of engagement."

295. Is the Movement opposed to the political, governmental or democratic system?

No. The fact that, as a thoroughly civic, autonomous initiative, the Movement is situated entirely *outside* the conventional channels of political representation – party, government, state, etc. – does not mean that it therefore stands in some way *against* the political, governmental or democratic system.

The non-profit-oriented management of its educational and cultural institutions distinguishes the Movement sharply from political actors and formal state institutions and agencies. Its forms of collective action do not contend for space with or in government or state institutions or agencies. They deal with human beings individually in the public space through independent, legally constituted civic organizations.

Hizmet's origin, source and target is the individual human being in the private sphere. The Movement's approach is "bottom–up", transforming individuals through education to consolidate a peaceful, harmonious and inclusive society as a result of an enlightened public sphere. It is not the "top–down" approach characteristic of state or government agency.

This reflects Gülen's rationale for the primacy of education among the Movement's commitments: "As the solution of every problem in this life ultimately depends on human beings, education is the most effective vehicle, regardless of whether we have a paralyzed social and political system or we have one that operates like clockwork."

296. Does the Movement intend to reduce or remove all differences among people and social systems?

The Movement equips people with cognitive, social, cultural and material resources to construct their present and future. It also equips them with the language to design their experience in all of its dimensions. The codes of behavior and services in the Movement enable people to make sense of their actions and to mediate between a plurality of conflicting demands and communities. The Movement does not attempt by its action to reduce or remove all specificities and irreducible differences among people and social systems; it intends to educate people to respect and benefit from those differences.

297. Why is it that Gülen and the Movement are still accused of being a "threat to the state"?

Even though Gülen has clearly stated and demonstrated that he has no political agenda, that he is against the instrumentalist use of religion in politics, that his emphasis is on the individual, the protectionist elite still, in a ritualized way, accuse him and the Movement of being a "threat to the state." The Australian researcher Greg Barton comments, "His critics, most of whom appear not to be very familiar with his writing and ideas, see him as promoting a different kind of Islam to that recognized and approved by the state. This apprehension is largely based on a false understanding. In fact Gülen is not so much advocating a different kind of Islam but rather an Islam that reaches more deeply into people's lives and transforms them to become not just better believers but better citizens."[7]

---

[7] G. Barton, Progressive Islamic thought, civil society and the Gülen movement in the national context: parallels with Indonesia. Paper presented at *Islam in the*

WHAT IS HIZMET'S RELATION TO CIVIC SOCIETY?

298. *Why is the Movement nowadays being classified as a civic initiative or civil society movement?*

Civil society is an arena of friendships and associations. It provides citizens with opportunities to learn the democratic habits of free assembly, non-coercive dialogue, and socio-economic initiative. It covers a broad array of organizations that are essentially private, that is, outside the institutional structures of government. These include voluntary associations that are beyond the household but outside the state.

For these reasons Hizmet is now best described as a civic initiative or a civil society movement that started as faith-initiated, non-contentious, cultural and educational service-projects. It is not a governmental or a state-sponsored organization. It is an apolitical, social, altruistic action. It centers on the individual, individual change and the education of the individual. Part of this education is also focused on raising consciousness about legality, lawfulness, human rights and one's constitutionally defined rights. It also works for the consolidation, therefore, of pluralist participatory democracy and equal rights.

The SMOs and institutions within Hizmet are civic initiatives that are also distinct from business organizations: they are not primarily commercial ventures set up principally to distribute profits to their directors or owners. Unlike other private institutions, they are set up to serve the public, not to generate profits for those involved in them. They are self-governing and people are free to join or support them voluntarily. They embody a commitment to freedom and personal initiative. They emphasize solidarity for service-projects and collectively organized altruism. They encourage and enable people to make full use of their legal rights of citizenship to act on their own authority so as to improve the quality of their own lives and the lives of others in general. They embody the idea or ideal that people have responsibilities not only to themselves but also to the communities of which they are a part.

Contemporary World: The Fethullah Gülen Movement in Thought and Action, Rice University, Texas, November 12–13, 2005, 9.

Within the legal space as given, the Movement combines private structure and public purpose, providing society with private institutions that are serving essentially public purposes. The institutions' connections to a great number of citizens and their multiple belonging and professionalized networks within the civil society sector, enhance the Movement's flexibility and capacity to encourage and channel private initiatives in support of public educational purposes and philanthropic services.

299. What makes Hizmet a "social altruistic action"?

Hizmet has an altruistic, social, purposive and collective orientation; social, because interactions are built on social relations, on a one-to-one basis, and defined by the interdependence and the meanings that tie people together; altruistic, because participants do not pursue personal, material and political ambitions; purposive, because individuals and groups act collectively to construct institutions by means of organized investments; and collective, because people define in cognitive and affective terms the field of possibilities and limits and simultaneously activate their resources and relationships to create meanings and services out of their joint behavior, and also mutually recognize them.

300. How does Hizmet contribute to the public space?

Whenever the collective action of Hizmet openly addresses the central issues affecting society, it redefines the public space. This process affects political life, everyday lives, mental codes, and interpersonal relationships. Hizmet, as a collective cultural action, symbolically reverses the *naming*, the way of interpreting our reality and experience, that is imposed on society by the dominant protectionist interests, and it reveals the arbitrariness of that *naming* or interpretation. It interprets and restructures reality using different perspectives, which lead to the crumbling of the minority's power to interpret reality for everyone else in a way that hurts or oppresses all those who are not part of the elite.

However, no sooner does Hizmet raise a new theme in the public sphere than it meets new limits. The mechanisms of the political system become selective, excluding and suppressing some of the dynamic components of the issue.

Nevertheless, some hopeful shifts in attitude have been observed, both in the political arena and among the general public as a whole. For example, as the Movement's discourse has gained influence through the visibility of its actions and platforms, there has been a change in the public perception of Islam. Previously, there had been efforts, in the service of short-sighted interests, to propagate and manipulate negative images of Islam. Yet, through the action of Hizmet, these images have gradually been modified.

301. As a civil society movement what is Hizmet's stance on religion and the state?

While the Movement's origin and services arise from a civil-society-based faith initiative, its discourse and practice affirm the idea that religion and the state are and can be separate in Islam, and that this does not endanger the faith but in fact protects it and its followers from exploitation and may strengthen it.

302. How does Hizmet enable citizens?

The Movement helps people to achieve their potential for autonomy and self-realization through a virtuous circle of mobility and exchange (of information, ideas and personnel) between the managers and the managed. There is a relationship between them of sustained mutual vigilance combined with mutual good faith and patience; they are willing, on occasions of unusual difficulty, to give each other the benefit of the doubt.

Hizmet tries to provide for this individual autonomy along with harmonious integration of complexity and multiplicity. In this way it helps to prevent exclusion and marginalization, and the fracturing of society into conflicting interest groups, all operating in a climate of distrust and hostility. So the Movement gives individuals a voice in the civil area, a virtuous circle reliably linking the state with its people, the managed with their managers. The Movement's positive service-ethic can be understood as an offer to mend the broken circle, to re-unite society, and to heal divisions between society and state.

Through its discourse and actions Hizmet has reawakened collective consciousness and directed attention to the radical social, cultural and spiritual dimensions of human needs, which the nation's politics systematically ignores or obscures. In Turkey this contrasts with the authoritarian elite's approach to the management of the nation's development which has been consistently exclusionary. The elite imposes an order and reality solely of its own making. It often expresses its interpretation of reality with impatient disdain for the doubts and reservations of anyone who is concerned about how the elite's imposed order causes a loss of cultural integrity and historical continuity.

303. How does Hizmet conduct its activities in civil society?

The Movement acts as a civic initiative with the moral duty to treat all others fairly and compassionately. It links collective goals and individual transformation and strives to retain respect for individual differences. It holds that altruistic service – in the way of education, health and welfare, interfaith dialogue and peace – is inherent to being a true Muslim and a true human being. To eradicate ignorance, arrogance, hostilities and gaps within and between societies, the Movement fosters voluntary forms of altruistic action.

304. What sort of outcomes does Hizmet have?

Hizmet is distinguished by its substantial and sustained contribution to the potential of citizens to apply their energies to discover and implement new solutions following their own development agendas. It has boosted voluntary participation, multiplied networks of committed citizens in mutually trusting relationships, pursuing through respectful dialogue and collaborative effort the shared goal of improving community services. As non-governmental organizations, Gülen-inspired schools contribute to the well-being and cultures of Turkey and other countries.

Hizmet's action yields new cultural, organizational and relational models, projects and responsibilities for the common good. It awakens in people the disposition to accommodate diversity and multiplicity, to reinforce solidarity and humane cooperation between different communities, and to contribute to civil, pluralist, democratic, healthy and peaceful societies.

The Movement is an agent for the accumulation of social capital. Benefiting from highly personal social relationships governed by the logic of SMOs, traditional solidarity, flexible thinking and dynamic impulse, Hizmet gives hope of achieving and preserving the meaning of human behavior along with the richness of diversity in a global society.

305. How does the Movement utilize the potential in civil society and reduce conflict?

The Movement has reawakened the force for change that was dormant at the roots of civil society. It has managed to embody this apolitical potential in institutions in order to advance education and thus to revitalize and consolidate civic, pluralist and democratic institutions. It has demonstrated that there are peaceful, non-confrontational, institutional channels for the handling of demands. It has opened new channels for individual and collective mobility, and this opening obstructs the formation of conflictual actions. Thus, Hizmet has acted as a barrier against actions that reduce everything produced in civil society to party politics and has prevented the public space from being manipulated for cheap political gains and games.

306. What underlies Hizmet's apparent strength?

Gülen and the Movement as collective actor have established links with already legitimized and institutionalized SMO leaders, communities and organizations. These links reinforce the prestige and legitimacy of the collective action, the actors and the SMOs of the Movement. This can be particularly helpful when the collective actor is forced to respond to crises or emergencies.

307. Does Hizmet use its strength to dominate Turkish political life or to exert undue influence on a whole social field?

No, quite the contrary. The Movement strives to perform a modernizing role within institutions and societies. It has contributed to the creation of common public spaces in which agreement can be reached to share the responsibility for a whole social field beyond one party's interests or positions. Greek Patriarch Bartholomew's comment confirms this: "In Turkey, Christians, Muslims and Jews live together in an atmosphere of tolerance and dialogue. We wish to mention the work of Fethullah Gülen, who more than ten years ago began to educate his believers about the necessity for the existence of a dialogue between Islam and all religions."[8]

The moral dimension of these issues and the successful provision of services that transcend any one party's interests or positions, raise awareness and so fuel reflection and discussion. This indicates a cultural change that is already under way in Turkey. Some militant secularists in the army and the old elite structure see this change as an assault on their interests, or an attempt to change the power relationships in the political system, and thereby to gain influence over political decisions.

However, in contrast to the action typical of an elite, Hizmet promotes an apolitical, highly tolerant and open regeneration of faith-inspired values, focused on education, democracy, tolerance and the formation of civil society. Participants and supporters of Hizmet are at ease with their Islamic heritage at the same time as taking part in a modern, technologically oriented society that is part of the global system.

---

[8] Bartholomew, Islam, Secularism and Democracy: The Turkish Experience. From the "Message of His All Holiness Ecumenical Patriarch Bartholomew to the Abant Platform". Washington DC, April 19–20, 2004, 4. Available from <www.sais-jhu.edu/mediastream/videoOndemand/PDF/ Bartholomew. pdf>.

NATURE OF THE COUNTER-MOBILIZATION

308. What has evoked hostility towards the Movement?

It is the success of the Movement's mobilization that has evoked considerable hostility in some quarters. Leaving aside envy, which is simply a psychological issue, there are a number of political, ideological, and financial factors motivating this hostility. First of all, *any* collective mobilization – not only or particularly Hizmet – that is not initiated by the protectionist groups within the power establishment is viewed with disfavor by the establishment; the establishment tends to regard any independent collective action as a potential threat to itself. If an independent collective mobilization proves its success or efficacy, the establishment mobilizes against it because the mobilization encroaches upon territory that vested interest groups within the establishment need to monopolize for their own purposes. Those in the establishment work to prevent or limit the action of the civic mobilization so that they can pursue their own projects and schemes and retain their hold on the levers of power.

Moreover, Hizmet's mobilization draws on cultural codes and traditions that the protectionist groups within the establishment in Turkey wish to suppress. The militant secularist elite prefers to represent Islam and Muslims to the public as radical and backward, but the discourse and action of Gülen and Hizmet does not permit the elite to successfully perpetuate in the public space that negative view of Islam and Muslims. In addition, Hizmet succeeds in educating huge numbers of people from outside the established elite by teaching them foreign languages and providing scholarships for study in foreign countries. This also makes the establishment feel threatened because they fear losing their control of the country and its resources. These factors explain why they particularly and very publicly chose to target Gülen himself and the Movement. They have targeted them as a smokescreen to distract public attention (and legal scrutiny) away from their own financial and ideological schemes.

In spite of the establishment's hostility, the Movement's projects and activities have educated and trained many thousands of people. Hizmet has provided people with moral orientation and guidance that makes them orderly, law-abiding citizens, an effort that has improved and modernized society, and widened opportunity. In doing all this, the Movement has systematically avoided contentious or adversarial action, so that its work should strengthen public order and social cohesion, and so that it should not be used (or construed) as a threat to the power or authority of the state and its institutions.

309. Exactly what kind of group or groups oppose the Movement?

The protectionist political elite within the Turkish establishment collaborates with the interest groups mostly formed out of the '68 generation (as it is known in Turkey). The experiences of that generation resulted in ideological readings of reality – dogmatism, separatism, sectarianism, violent clashes and armed conflict – that still haunt and prevent the elite's thinking from keeping abreast of the changing terms of social, economic and political realities in Turkey.

The statist, elitist, leftist, militant secularists, ultra- and neo-nationalists in Turkey failed to produce either political ideas or the tools with which ideas can be put into practice. They failed to deliver, in other words, not just an alternative point of view but also the means whereby it could be made practicable. They were unable to produce a political design that comprised instruments and models of transformation compatible with the historical, economic, and social context. Also, the effects of their actions at the systemic level did not enable cultural innovation or institutional modernization. That inability has reduced them to an ineffectual "opposition" in the Turkish Parliament and a minority voice in the wider society; their position and programs are mostly articulated and projected from within the Republican People's Party, or simply "the left" in Turkey. These groups have contributed little to the development of reflexivity in the larger societal context or social cohesion. Their ideologies and action have become a means and source of polarization, segmentation and tension in Turkey.

310. Why did those groups counter-mobilize against Gülen and the Movement?

The dominant protectionist group assume that social, cultural and political representation in Turkey, as well as the identification of any societal problems and their solution, are their sole and exclusive prerogative. This is best seen in their counter-mobilization during the *February 28 Process* against SMOs and civil society. The counter-mobilization was not based on democratic procedures or political consensus but was, and still is, realized and secured through ideological interpretation. The protectionist system propagates itself and permeates daily life and existential choices. It filters and represses some demands by presenting them as an absolute, existential threat to the very structure of society. When the dominant group cannot compete with any alternative in argument, action and services, it uses the protectionist system to stigmatize any suggestion or advice, any alternative or opposition, as a threat to national security.

Despite the fact that such interpretation and counter-mobilization is anti-democratic and anti-egalitarian, the protectionist elite legitimates it by exploiting combinations of events and circumstances and segmentation, radicalization and tension in society.

The counter-mobilization also resurfaces at different times and in different circumstances as improprieties, corruption or concealment of other vested interests. One way for protectionist actors to seek a reduction in the risks involved in a decision is to secure for themselves a preventive consensus through the use of ideological manipulation. This preventive consensus usually goes by the name of "Kemalism" in Turkey.

The counter-mobilization in Turkey has in practice decayed into a counter-mobilization against all except themselves. It is especially targeted at religion, religious people, and all modernizing efforts and projects originating from the faith-inspired communities. That is the context of their making Gülen and the Movement their major "adversary."

311. Why are Gülen's views perceived by such groups to pose a threat?

Views in favor of the consolidation of democratic and basic human rights in Turkey are repressed on account of the threat they are perceived to pose to the structural advantage of the dominant protectionist interests in society. So Gülen's views are seen as implicitly calling into question the privileges of those interests in utilizing political processes and questioning the protectionists' hegemony over the political system. The protectionists fear that certain understandings and demands may alter the balance of the political system and financial interests and may cause the criteria for selection and entry into that system to be widened.

312. How do the protectionists in Turkey act against civil society initiatives and services?

The protectionist groups are apprehensive that they might lose their direct control over power and their collective vested interests within the system, so they direct their aggression at Hizmet at least partly in order to repair this loss in the eyes of the general public and their supporters. They do this to show that they are still the masters and owners of all in Turkey. They believe it is their prerogative to think and act in this way. They therefore do not respect and recognize anyone else who is successful and influential in the public space, or who affects mentalities and attitudes in Turkey and guides people.

The protectionist groups have a common interest in keeping the system closed as far as possible. They react predictably to hold on to their established position within that system by resisting alternative initiatives and projects. Benefitting from the legal vagueness and the cohorts they have developed and installed within the judiciary and military, they counter-mobilize against civil society and the consolidation of constitutional and participative democracy. They see freedoms, rights and alternative ideas that arise from civil society outside their cliques and clubs as excessive, unnecessary, and a threat to the System. Under the guise of safeguarding secularism and the System, they have always sought to reduce everything produced in civil society to political in-fighting, threats or manipulation.

As a result, when mutual recognition and respect breaks down, their aggressive feelings gain prominence and are redirected onto their "adversary." The protectionist groups, which are in decline within the political system and which have lost the esteem of the overwhelming majority of the masses they despise, showed clearly in the presidential election in 2007 and the related discussions and in the process of making constitutional reform or amendments that they have a common interest in keeping the system closed as far as possible. They react predictably to hold on to their established position within that system by resisting the intended outcome. They counter-mobilize against civil society – in this case, against Hizmet. Wherever it is possible for them to do so, they impose selective and exclusionary restrictions on the criteria for social movement ventures and services.

Examples of the selective and exclusionary restrictions they imposed include the imposition of co-ed schooling even in the private school system; blocking access to certain departments in higher education for vocational school graduates, especially those from Imam Hatip (religious training) schools; banning qualified women who wear a headscarf from state and public institutions and public space; blacklisting and boycotting private companies run by business people from the faith communities; blacklisting certain newspapers and reporters; and dismissals of military and judicial personnel who do not appear to support the protectionist ideology and protect its adherents from legal action.

313. Is Hizmet marginal in any way?

The Movement is rightly considered to be marginal in aspiring to access to the political system. It is also receives very little in the way of positive social recognition from the very small, yet highly influential, protectionist elite and state bureaucracy. However, there is no automatic or univocal correlation between that protectionist elite and the people, the electing many. As evidenced by the disclosure of many planned and attempted coups, the elite uses a "strategy of tension," that is, fear, propaganda, disinformation, psychological warfare, *agents provocateurs* and false flag terrorism in an attempt to control and manipulate public opinion so as to mask its own huge financial and political power and conceal its agenda to maintain its own power. This is also known in Turkey as "the state security syndrome." These mechanisms of intervention and control in the public space then restrict the development of civil society, of collective experience and services in Turkey including (but not uniquely) those of Hizmet.

However, since Hizmet is a non-ideological, inclusive, grassroots, mass movement, in real terms it is not at all marginal. It is in fact much more representative of society as a whole than the countermobilization, which is a small, protectionist elite with a very specific ideology that does not appeal to or represent the masses.

314. Why have some voices in Turkey objected to Gülen's interfaith dialogue activities?

In democracy in general people are encouraged to participate in order to have a voice. However, despite the fact that Turkey is a democratic country, if and when someone other than one of the established actors within the political system does achieve something, the pervasive tendency of the protectionist groups is to start calling for silence, retreat, and isolation. Alternatively, they may try to co-opt the other actor into their fold, rather than supporting communication, inclusion and socialization. They require people to accept the place that the dominant ideology assigns to them and accept the values of the dominant protectionist codes. So, when Gülen has met with presidents, premiers, ministers, or other officials or authorities, local or foreign, the reaction of the vested interest groups has been vocal and contentious. To them, Gülen's place is to be a "mere preacher" who must lead prayers but do nothing more. They do not want to understand why he finds himself dealing with cultural and social issues, or why he was accepted as a partner in dialogue by world leaders, such as the late Pope John Paul II, and why others continue to pursue dialogue with him.

315. What was the "West Working Group" and why did it target Hizmet?

The West Working Group was a group set up initially within the Turkish Armed Forces (TSK); it was subsequently abolished or modified into various tactical units. The West Working Group interfered with politics and governance and became a unit that planned anti-democratic schemes and putsch-like events. (Since the group was disbanded, its members have resurfaced in warfare units in the TSK that have continued to plot strategies for coup attempts.) The group claimed its name epitomized its adherence to Western values because Westernization is one of the fundamental principles of the Turkish Republic.

However, the members' actions gave the lie to their words: the task of safeguarding democracy means playing the democratic game to its fullest extent: it means demanding that all political players make the reasons for their positions and policies known to the public; it means ensuring that "the rules of the game" are respected; it means struggling against the monopolization of information; it means opposing government policies constructively by offering credible alternative policies. It means also that the autonomy of civil society actors must be respected. Their concerns must not be collapsed into the political arena; rather, political actors and society in general must acknowledge and respect the distance that civil society actors maintain from the political arena.

Regrettably, the culture of this and similar special interest groups was, on *February 28* during the period of the *post-modern coup* and subsequent intervention, ill-prepared to undertake the task of safeguarding democracy, for those groups have always sought to reduce everything produced in civil society to political in-fighting, threats or manipulation. The Turkish public now sees that interest groups embodied in such units as the West Working Group do not care at all about Western values. The Group's members are dreaming of a West devoid of democratization, individual rights, human rights, freedom of worship and civil initiative.

EFFICACY OF HIZMET

316. Why is Hizmet seen as a successful social movement?

The Movement has proved itself successful in the sight of communities in Turkey and abroad by mobilizing inactive, dormant, but innovative energies present in Turkish society and other societies. It absorbs conflicting pressures and eases tension within fragmented communities. It has transformed the potential to use coercive means to induce changes in political systems into peaceful efforts to produce beneficial services. Despite provocations and ill-treatment, it has never shown any inclination whatever towards violence or extra-legal tactics of any kind.

317. How does the Movement gain support and from whom?

The Movement progressively modernizes its culture and organization. Along with support from the grassroots for the services provided, it connects with and gains support from influential people such as community leaders and industrialists, as well as small businessmen. By employing a sound rationality through the obvious neutrality of technical expertise, it is able to appeal to all. It socializes and transmits values and rules in order to oversee the development of personal and holistic skills.

318. Where does the strength of the Movement come from?

Hizmet's action is capable of bridging the rifts modernization generates. Through its work the coordinates of meaning, action and serving have been transformed; it proclaims a change which equally entails a change of the self. It affirms a non-contentious difference but does not renounce the validity of other perspectives or rationality. In this lies the strength of the Movement.

319. What accounts for the efficacy of Hizmet as a collective actor?

Hizmet is composed of many SMOs pursuing similar goals but different strategies. While no one owns the services and authority in the name of the collective actor, Hizmet guarantees its participants access to immediate and verifiable control of the goods and services organized through their collective action. The Movement is strengthened by flexibility, adaptability and immediacy and by its availability as a channel for the direct expression of needs that state organizations, political parties or other more structured organizations cannot incorporate.

The Movement's collective action and its institutions have a number of obvious strengths: the institutions' ability to pursue general goals over the long term; their insusceptibility to escapism, extremism or violence; the simplicity of their decision making and mediation; their efficiency and effectiveness, and their work ethic in which a variety of interests collaborate. Thus, the organization and effectiveness of the SMOs of Hizmet, and their service ethic all contribute to its efficacy as a complex collective actor.

320. How is the use of participants' skills maximized?

The Movement has formed a large number of organizations operating across economic, political and cultural boundaries. It circulates and diffuses ideas, information, new patterns of action and cultures. In this way, it is able to transfer latency into visibility through collective action and services, which are then institutionalized. Through media and publications, workshops, public forums and conferences, as well as through visits to other institutions, service networks and different regions of the world, the Movement participants harmoniously integrate and liaise between its many layers, formally and informally, as the need arises.

321. What makes the SMOs leading institutions in their fields inside and outside Turkey?

The interweaving of the service-project mentality with different integrative strategies makes the SMOs successful. What makes them leading institutions in their field inside and outside of Turkey is that employment is based on specialized training and on formal certification organized and issued by the States where participants are active. Employment and advancement is in accord with knowledge, achievement and professional expertise and competence rather than seniority or preference given to friends and relatives. In the SMOs, which are institutionalized and professionalized – for example, the educational institutions, hospitals or the media – there are paid staff who are not active in the voluntary aspect of the Movement's activities but are nevertheless broadly sympathetic to its aims, and individuals from the grassroots of the Movement who are pursuing a career in those SMOs.

322. What makes decision taking efficient in Hizmet?

Notably within the social organization or production of the service-networks of the Movement, the efficiency of decision taking is explained by the constancy and richness of the interaction of many individuals, its being multi-scaled and across multiple affiliations. This results in adaptive, spontaneous, self-organizing networks with representative leaders generated from the grassroots, from "bottom-up."

323. Where does the strength or efficacy of the service networks come from?

Networks are the basis on which movements are built, and they perform different kinds of functions – as means of teaching people about the values of the movement, of reinforcing social cohesion or solidarity, of exchanging information and of organizing activities.

In Hizmet's service-networks there are no written rules, no fixed procedures, no formal leadership and there is no fixed structure of bureaus. Authority comes from the collective decision taking. Decisions on what to do are taken locally or in an individual project-network. The networks attract supporters or adherents who are often more committed than those who have formal membership of political parties, and the efficacy resulting from this commitment is what gives service networks strength and efficacy.

However, as Hizmet becomes an organic part of society in some fields, it crystallizes into a professional structure. Formal organization brings disciplined participation and coordination of strategies for achieving the Movement's aims. In fact, Hizmet is a successful combination of both informal service networks and institutionalized services, such as aid and relief organizations, schools and dialogue societies, in which everything is registered and by fixed and written rules and procedures and regulations; some service fields naturally require informal networks and people and their unregistered contribution, some necessitate formalized, institutionalized networks, and some require both.

As for the management of formalized structures, all the institutions in Hizmet are independent corporate bodies. There is no formal relationship among educational institutions or the other institutions, both within and outside Turkey, except where there is a chain run by an educational or charitable trust. However, the institutions do disperse news of their accomplishments through the mass media and promotions. In this way, ideas and thoughts that arise from a commitment to the same feelings can be shared and owned by all.

324. How do the participants become so committed to the Movement?

Evidence shows that the more closely the individual is integrated into a group, the greater will be the degree of her or his participation. Participation is an expression of belonging to a certain social group, and the more secure the affiliation is, the more intense the participation. Then, the more intense the collective participation in a network of relations, the more rapid and durable will be the mobilization of a movement or its SMOs. This seems to be the case in Hizmet's service-networks. The Movement facilitates and thus increases an individual's willingness to get involved in service-projects through her or his relationship with a larger group of like-minded, similarly intentioned people.

325. How successful is the Movement in convincing people to make philanthropic contributions?

Using its accommodative, service-solidarity, organizational skills and the trust it has earned from the people, the Movement has been extraordinarily successful at convincing the public to use its constitutionally given rights to serve humanity positively, constructively, and through self-motivated philanthropic contributions and charitable trusts. For this reason, the Movement has become a vital component in providing an alternative and barrier to egoistic interests at the expense of others and a remedy for societal discord, conflict and violence. It is now one of the most significant and leading actors in the renewal process towards a civil, pluralist, democratic and peaceful society in Turkey.

326. What does participation yield for participants?

Responding to the call to take part enables people, through different channels, to experience a passionate optimism: they want to experience now what it is possible to accomplish; they want to do whatever is beneficial and meaningful for others and for coming generations. What is done on a small scale in one context creates meaning and repercussions within a broader compass. What people engage in may appear not to affect themselves directly, but it feeds and promotes something essential for the collective actor. It enables the actor to realize an effective mobilization or rapid and widespread diffusion of a service-project through multiple affiliations.

327. How are local forms of action able to exert influence beyond their local effect?

Altruism is elevated to a virtue of the highest standing in Hizmet. The relationship of the individual to the others acting in the collectivity is encouraged and built in togetherness with others. This attitude implies different work ethics: gratuitousness, coordinated and effective services towards common goals, personal sacrifice in the interest of humanity, and working hard in the present for a happy future. Through interdependence and co-operation with all, and through the diffusion and proliferation of informational and educational institutions, Hizmet renders seemingly weak, insignificant and local forms of action potentially able to exert an enormous influence far beyond their actual size and local effect.

328. What are the sources of the beliefs and values of the Movement?

The sources and resources of the Movement are education, cultural experience and awareness, religious consciousness through knowledge and study, participation in social and communitarian representative bodies, responsibility and altruism, and belief in societal accord, peace, democracy, and co-operation (as opposed to clash) between civilizations.

329. How does the Movement learn and develop?

The Movement has involved diverse people within a very short time over a large geographical area to achieve joint projects. It appears to have established the ideal balance between risks and advantages, so that millions of people are taking part in service-projects. Movement participants recognize the outcomes of its actions and secure positive recognition from others. In this way, participants can compare and perceive Hizmet's consistency and continuity over time and across borders. By comparing their investments with the results of their actions, they can relate the rewards to the resources invested in the action, and make rational decisions about the best way to make future investments of resources and efforts.

330. How does the Movement enable people to become reflexive and beneficial to others?

By prioritizing knowledge and education rather than party politics or partisanship, Hizmet enables people to make better use of their resources, to free themselves from material and other inequalities, and to become reflexive and beneficial to others. Gülen teaches that for a better future, humanity needs more tolerant and more altruistic individuals with magnanimous hearts and genuinely open minds which respect freedom of thought, which are open to science and scientific research, and which look for the harmony between the Divine law and life.

331. What is "reflexivity" exactly and why is Hizmet described as "reflexive"?

An action is said to generate "reflexivity" if it enables individuals, within the limits set at any given moment by the environment, to recognize the forces of socialization on them and to alter their place in the social structure. They can affirm and express their autonomy, their being different from other actors within a system, and they can own, produce and represent to others the meaning of their action. That meaning is distinct from the specific content of the action itself and constitutes the collective identity. It is enhanced by belonging to organizational and communications networks because such networks yield solidarity and build resistance against impositions (of identity or meaning) from above by remote, impersonal powers.

The reflexivity of Hizmet is very high, as its collective identity is not based on primary associations such as gender, age, locality, ethnicity or religion. Instead, it is based on projects and services for the common and collective good. Reflexivity is both the product and the cause of collective action; it is created in the midst of collective actions, and the process of maintaining it stimulates further collective action.

332. How does Hizmet establish continuity between the individual and collectivity?

The service-networks and the individuals who participate in the networks see their own limitations through face-to-face discussions, through availability of information and communication channels, through skilled leadership in SMOs, through the feedback from media and public, and through consultation. This makes them reflexive.

By generalizing and accumulating the results of their actions, the service-networks and SMOs relate to society and express people's wishes and concerns through peaceful and formal mechanisms. In this way they contribute to finding institutional solutions to individual and collective needs, expectations and interests. In short, Hizmet is an institutional intermediary between the individual and the collectivity or society.

This yields continuity between individual and collective identity, leisure and commitment, self-fulfillment and participation, particular and global.

333. How is continuity achieved in the Movement?

In Hizmet there is continuity between individual and collective identity, and between leisure and commitment. This continuity arises out of the nature of people's participation, commitment and personal fulfillment. Participants belong to many, varying and overlapping networks of relations. In these network relations, individual needs and collective goals, and individual and collective interests are constantly negotiated and served. Individuality and collectivity are therefore not mutually exclusive. While the individual and diverse contributions enrich community, ultimately individuals also benefit from what is done for and to the wider community. Also, people commit themselves to service-projects both within leisure time and working time. The continuity between leisure and commitment presupposes a close connection between self-fulfillment and participation, and enhances a great deal of feeling and meaning.

The joint effort of Hizmet as a collective actor with the other groups or organizations in wider society, and the combination of service or vocation with professionalism are also factors that give continuity to the Movement. Thus there is continuity of relationship between individual and community, between the Movement and society, between the past and the present, between the Movement's goals and universal values, between the particular, local goals and issues the Movement deals with and the global concerns of the people of the world. This continuity is strengthened by the Movement's observing the legal and normal boundaries wherever it works, and affirming its citizenship in the System: its respect for legal boundaries secures for Hizmet attitudinal support for its values and goals.

334. How is diffusion facilitated in the Movement?

The rapid and widespread diffusion of Hizmet's ideas and practices throughout the world has been facilitated by the multiple affiliations of participants in Hizmet. Diffusions can be either direct or indirect depending on whether they come about through direct contacts between participants or are mediated by the mass media. Cultural representations and news coverage shape the practices of other participants through diffusion, so that even when they share no network connections, participants learn about Movement innovations, actions and successes through the mass media.

The Movement has spread beyond Turkish national borders, developing contemporaneously and displaying significant similarities in different countries. Diffusion has been strongest in the neighboring countries, which are geographically and culturally close, but it is also very strong in others with no historical ties or similarities in social and political structure. Hizmet's peaceful cultural–educational and collaborative understanding brings different social actors and institutions together around common meanings and values. Diffusion has occurred through personal orientations, literature, conferences, the media, aid and relief agencies, educational and cultural SMOs, interfaith and dialogue organizations, and travel and visits.

The Movement does not attempt diffusion through recruitment among strangers, in private places, or by means of door-to-door canvassing.

335. How successful is Hizmet in changing public attitudes?

To date Hizmet has achieved some significant results in changing public attitudes. Through educational initiatives, new media organs and networks, opposition to violent and coercive means and methods, intercultural and interfaith dialogue, and co-operation on projects and services, Hizmet has succeeded in producing new projects and services that reveal the social and political nature of the definitions previously imposed by the dominant interest groups and their apparatuses.

Gülen and the Movement bring to the surface and act towards the elaboration of a neglected side of human experience: the need for meaning. The message of the Movement is embedded in its actions. While it generally does not ask for goods, advantages, or reforms, it nevertheless brings these forward by making visible new meaning through its practices and services.

The Movement presents society with cultural gifts through its actions: it reveals new possibilities, another face of reality. When it acts, something has been said by that action – a message has been incorporated into the social arena, and a transforming debate can get under way. Hizmet's effort is perceived by the protectionist forces as a challenge to the powers within the establishment. Whether or not the messages of Hizmet's action become topics for political contestation depends on how far they are taken up (or not) by politically relevant agents and how far they become political agendas for the public. Regardless, the Movement proves itself capable of bringing about a change in the way people's experiences are perceived and defined or *named*. Thus, it becomes the bearer of the hidden potential for change, and it announces new possibilities to the rest of society.

336. How does Hizmet maintain continuity at the same time as progress and advancement?

Hizmet stresses reality and service-projects not an/the actor. As the Movement establishes itself here and now with projects, and as it establishes its location, consistency, commitment and trust, it gives people hope to think about the future. Hizmet does not oppose the idea that people should retain their values while changing; it reinforces the idea that retaining values and maintaining permanence does not need to contradict continuity, progress and advancement. This factor attracts many individuals into service-networks and projects.

337. Why have the models proposed and established by the Movement survived?

When new understandings are widely acknowledged and welcomed, and when people rapidly institutionalize for societal needs and cultural projects, this gives rise to new social models. The models provided by Hizmet are cultural rather than political, they transform patterns of thought and relationship. These models survive because they follow a lawful political and institutional form. The Movement has achieved rapid transformation of attitudes, efficient institutionalization of public needs and initiatives, collective or organized philanthropy for education, and apparently simple solutions to societal discord which were previously lacking in Turkish society, and which were never attempted by the protectionist political bureaucracy.

338. What keeps Hizmet's autonomous networks together so that they are one movement?

The managerially distinct networks communicate their experiences with each other and with the wider public that they serve. Information, know-how, and patterns of behavior circulate, passing from one network to another, and bringing a degree of homogeneity to the whole. The service-networks thus differ radically from the image of the politically organized actor. Service groups operate on their own, not from one center, although they maintain links to the collective actor through the circulation of information and professionalized people in the fabric of daily life.

339. If Hizmet is not oppositional, how can it be effective as a social movement?

Hizmet has systematically shunned contentious, political or direct action, preferring to remain, in principle and practice, non-adversarial. Instead, in order to consolidate and revitalize democratic processes, participants have exerted themselves in constructive efforts to draw contending individuals and groups to collaborate in a common spirit of service. A prominent example of these efforts is their establishment in Turkey of the Journalists and Writers Foundation (JWF) and the Abant Platforms, a series of think tanks which successfully bring together academics, scholars, statesmen, and journalists who hold different, even conflicting, worldviews.

340. What effect does the Movement's mobilization have on segmentation in Turkish society?

It says much for the Movement's reflexivity, and its success in weakening or removing barriers between people, that it has enabled even those who have no part in its work to reflect on the irrational polarization, rigid separation and closure between different collective entities in Turkish society. The term used to denote such polarization is segmentation.

Hizmet's positive and constructive action acts as a bulwark against segmentation, polarization and alienation and disintegration in a complex society. The Movement's educational and cultural project-networks and service-networks help to increase social mobility. Through the media it gives people access to information and a wide variety of opinions and contributes to keeping society properly informed on social and cultural issues and developments.

In its own discourse and action it is never contentious or conflictual and consistently lays stress on transparency, lawfulness and legality.

When political actors cause societal tension, Hizmet's discourse is calming and urges seeking consensus on vital issues relating to the public and common good.

Hizmet is open to and encourages others to be open to alternative initiatives and liaison between like-minded peaceful civil actors. Last but not least the Movement helps to keep youth, the most fervent, volatile and easily provoked group in any society away from tensions, clashes and violence.

GLOSSARY

- *counter-mobilization*: used in this study to refer to the systematic efforts by the *protectionist elitists* to oppose the activities of all civil society movements in Turkey, and in particular the Gülen Movement.
- *dominant interests*: the interests of the *elitist-statist-secularist* group who wield power in Turkey, not always from behind the political stage.
- *elitists*: those who believe in their inherent superiority over others with an unquestionable right to pre-eminence, privilege and power. In Turkey, the *elitists* are the traditional Republican clique who define themselves as superior because of their "Western" cultural preferences and practices, education, attitudes, etc. Their assumption is that these Western qualities give them a greater right to govern, if necessary by overturning the will of the people.
- *February 28 Process*: to the sequence of measures and events that followed the *soft coup* of 1997: "On the last day of February 1997, the regular monthly meeting of the military-dominated National Security Council [...] gave the Welfare-True Path coalition government a list of eighteen measures to be implemented without delay, including a clampdown on 'reactionary Islam'. [...] The military spent the next months waging a relentless public-relations campaign that turned society against the government and eventually forced the resignation on June 18 of Erbakan and his cabinet. The noose on civilian politics remained tight after that. Press freedom was severely curtailed, with many journalists and other public figures targeted by military-orchestrated smear campaigns. [...] What is called within Turkey 'the February 28 process' was not limited to the political wing of the Islamist movement. Islamic networks, sects, associations, and individuals were targeted for excoriation and sometimes prosecution or court-ordered bans on their activities."[9]
- *hizmet*: word of Arabic origin (literally, "service"), used in Turkish to mean disinterested voluntary beneficial service to others, especially pro-

[9] Özel, S. (2003) After the Tsunami. *Journal of Democracy* 14(2), 80–94: 87.

vided by faith-inspired communities; the preferred term among participants in the Gülen Movement to describe their attitude and work.

- *Islamic*: adjectival form, referring to the traditional teachings of the religion, and expressly distinguished from *Islamist*.
- *Islamism*, *Islamist*: politically motivated understanding among Muslim activists who believe in evolutionary or revolutionary transformation in society and political systems; Islam understood as ideology.
- *laicism*: a militant (Jacobin) form of *secularism* that demands the exclusion of religious belief and practice from public life, and expects to use state power to achieve that exclusion. In Turkey until recently there has been little real distinction between *laicism* and *secularism*.[10]
- *mobilization*: used in this book to refer to the efforts of the participants in the Gülen Movement to direct resources to achieve their goals in the form of service-projects.
- *National Security Council (NSC)*: a council of state consisting of the President, Prime Minister, a number of other ministers (as necessary and relevant to the issues being discussed), five top-ranking generals from the Chief of Staff, plus other generals (the number of generals always exceeding the number of civilians on the council). The purpose of the *NSC* is to advise the government on matters of national security, though its remit has gradually been extended to cover other aspects of Turkish public life, such as finance and culture.
- *postmodern coup*: see *soft coup*
- *protectionists*: those in the established leadership of Turkey with a strict nationalist, *secularist* and bureaucratic-authoritarian understanding who intend to perpetuate the status quo.
- *secularism*: legal and institutional separation of church and state, which, is understood to mean the separation/expulsion of religious authority from the state. In practice in Turkey, *secularism* means regulation by the state, to a considerable extent, of the practice of religion through the Presidency of Religious Affairs (appointment of prayer leaders to mosques, vetting content of sermons, religious education, etc.). The term *secularist* is widely used in Turkey to describe those who are actively opposed to religious practice in the public sphere – see *laicism* – and is so used in this book.

---

[10] "In fact, Turkish secularism derives from the radical Jacobin laicism that aims to transform society through the power of the state and eliminate religion from the public sphere." Berkes, N. 1998. *The Development of Secularism in Turkey*. New York: Routledge.

- *Social Movement Organization (SMO)*: any formally established and institutionalized organization whose operations and goals coincide with the preferences of a social movement.
- *soft coup*: in February 1997, the newly elected government of Turkey was induced to resign by an open threat from a select group of generals at the Turkish Chief of Staff of a military coup. The government stood down and the military assumed control of the civil authority of the state. The *soft coup* has sometimes been referred to also as the "postmodern coup."
- *statism, statists*: the doctrine that the state in Turkey should hold control of the major part of political and economic activity in the country and that this control should remain in the hands of the Republican *elitists*.
- *Sunnah*: normative way of life for Muslims, based on the teachings and practices of the Prophet Muhammad (pbuh) and on sound exegesis of the Qur'an.
- *symbolic challenge*: the production of new meanings, new social relations and services, which point up failures in state policy or inadequacies in the worldview of the *dominant interests*. (Different from physical or political challenge, which directly confronts the legitimacy of the authority of the state or its agents.)
- *vested interests*: the privileged group who currently enjoy financial and status benefits from the political and economic status quo in Turkey, and who are determined to hold on to their privileges by any means (including association with organized crime) and whatever the cost to the people or the society.

FURTHER READING

Carroll, B. Jill. *A Dialogue of Civilizations: Gülen's Islamic Ideals and Humanistic Discourse*. Somerset, New Jersey: The Light & The Gülen Institute, 2007.

Çetin, Muhammed. *The Gülen Movement: Civic Service without Borders*. New York: Blue Dome Press, 2009.

Ebaugh, Helen Rose. *The Gülen Movement: A Sociological Analysis of a Civic Movement Rooted in Moderate Islam*. New York: Springer, 2010.

Esposito, John L. and Ihsan Yilmaz. *Islam and Peacebuilding: Gülen Movement Initiatives*. New York: Blue Dome Press, 2010.

Gülen, Fethullah. "A Comparative approach to Islam and Democracy." *SAIS Review* 21 (2001): 133–8.

———. *Toward a Global Civilization of Love and Tolerance*. Somerset, New Jersey: The Light, 2004.

———. An interview with Gülen by Zeki Sarıtoprak & Ali Ünal. *The Muslim World Special Issue*, 95:3 (2005), 447–67.

———. *The Statue of Our Souls: Revival in Islamic Thought and Activism*.

Somerset, New Jersey: The Light, 2005.

Harrington, James C. *Wrestling with Free Speech, Religious Freedom, and Democracy in Turkey: The Political Trials and Times of Fethullah Gülen*. Lanham, Maryland: University Press of America, 2011.

Hunt, R. A. & Aslandogan, Y. A. eds. *Muslim Citizens of the Globalized World: Contributions of the Gülen Movement*. Somerset, New Jersey: IID Press & The Light, 2007.

Kalyoncu, M. *A Civilian Response to Ethno-Religious Conflict: The Gülen Movement in Southeast Turkey*. Clifton, New Jersey: Tughra Books, 2008.

INDEX

Q

R

S

T

U

V

W

Y

Z